Color from the Heart

SEVEN GREAT WAYS TO MAKE QUILTS WITH COLORS YOU LOVE

Gai Perry

C&T PUBLISHING

©1999 Gai Perry
Illustrations ©1999 C&T Publishing, Inc.

Editor: Liz Aneloski
Technical Editor: Lynn Koolish
Copy Editor: Vera Tobin
Cover and Book Designer: Aliza Kahn
Design Director: Diane Pedersen
Illustrator: Aliza Kahn
Photographer: Sharon Risedorph
Front Cover Photo: Heart's Delight by Gai Perry
Back Cover Photos: Family Values by Gai Perry
                  Climbing the Walls by Gai Perry
Published by C&T Publishing, Inc., P.O. Box 1456, Lafayette, California 94549

Attention Teachers:
C&T Publishing, Inc. encourages you to use this book as a text for teaching. Contact us at 800-284-1114 or www.ctpub.com for more information about the C&T Teachers Program.

Library of Congress Cataloging-in-Publication Data

Perry, Gai
Color from the heart : seven great ways to make quilts with colors you love / Gai Perry.
p. cm.
Includes bibliographical references (p.   ) and index.
ISBN 1-57120-071-1 (soft cover)
1. Patchwork quilts—Design. 2. Color in textile crafts. I. Title.
TT835 .P449114 1999
746.46—dc21   99-06063
   CIP

Printed in Hong Kong
10 9 8 7 6 5 4 3 2 1

ACKNOWLEDGEMENTS
I would like to extend my deepest gratitude and appreciation to all the terrific ladies who made quilts for this book. They didn't know, when they innocently signed up to take my color class, they would be asked to finish their quilts in record time in order to meet a publishing deadline. My thanks to all of you for being such good sports!

CONTENTS

FOREWORD

Quilting is an emotional joy ride. It can be soothing, stimulating, frustrating, rewarding...but never dull! It's also an oasis; an island of healing amidst a chaotic schedule of work, car pools, and care giving. Women turn to quiltmaking for all sorts of reasons. For some it's an expression of art. For others it's a forum in which to make a moral or political statement. Still others make quilts as a way of communicating love to a family member or friend. I used to paint pictures and I guess it should come as no surprise that so many artists find their way to quiltmaking. It's such an extraordinary experience to physically hold a color in one's hand; to cut into it and feel its body and texture. If you are familiar with my quilts, you have probably read one of my books and know that working with color is one of my greatest pleasures.

I had just finished writing the text for *Impressionist Palette* when I was asked to put together a show of my earlier, more traditional quilts. It seemed like a nice idea, so I went on a treasure hunt, culling old quilts from the backs of closets and blanket chests. I chose twenty of my favorite pieces and titled the show "Traditional Quilts Remembered."

The positive viewer response caught me by surprise. Apparently the quilt community had forgotten (or didn't know) I'd spent several years making traditional style quilts. I started getting requests for patterns and teaching dates. Unfortunately, the Impressionist Landscape Workshops were taking all my time, but it was nice to know traditional quilting was alive and well, and I was flattered by the attention my early work was generating.

Eight months later I was still thinking about those quilts. Seeing them on display had been like visiting with old friends. Eventually, the desire to renew the acquaintance became so overwhelming, I revived my traditional color classes and began making a few quilts that were totally unrelated to the Impressionist Landscape style.

I'm sure there must be a line in an old song that goes something like "everything old is new again." That's exactly the way I feel about traditional piecing right now. This past year of teaching and writing has been like a breath of fresh air. Sharing what I know about color with a new generation of quilters has made me consciously define the process I go through when choosing a palette of fabrics. I've come to realize that even though I've read and memorized most of what has been written about color theory, when it comes right down to it, *I choose colors with my heart, not my intellect.*

INTRODUCTION

This workbook is going to show you how to make quilts with colors you love! Perhaps, at one time or another, some of you have taken a class from a quilt teacher who suggested experimenting with your least favorite palette in order to stretch your color tolerance. I don't agree with this philosophy because I think if you work with colors that aren't personally stimulating, it's a pretty good bet you're not going to like the finished quilt. To me, it makes more sense to focus on colors you love and learn to put them in the best possible light.

Color from the Heart is not about traditional color theory.
So many quilt books about color are based on the artist's concept of harmony and contrast, but have you ever wondered if these rules need to be applied to quiltmaking? Should we really care about analogous and tertiary color schemes? Will we even remember what they are five minutes after reading about them? The answer is no, we probably won't remember, and yes, we should care, but for quilters, color theory is just the beginning.

We also need to concern ourselves with "fabric personality" (the message a particular fabric conveys). If you were making a contemporary wallhanging with brightly colored, abstract fabrics and you tried to include some traditional looking plaids or stripes, the impact of the contemporary design would be diluted and the viewer would get a mixed message. If you are serious about quiltmaking, you must learn to give color and fabric personality equal importance. This book will show you how to effectively combine these two elements.

A third element to be considered is "intuitive color choice": the ability to know when the colors and fabrics you're working with feel right. Intuition is an inherent gift and I like to define it as subconscious knowledge, or more simply stated, everything a person learns and then forgets. Here is an example. You know red and green look good together. You may or may not know they are also complementary colors which, according to color theory guidelines, are a dynamite combination. Intuition or knowledge? The way you know isn't important. What really matters is that you end up working with color combinations that are visually attractive and personally appealing. As you work through the lessons, you will be able to rely more and more on your intuitive color choices and less on other peoples' opinions of what looks right.

There are seven lessons in this workbook and each explores a different, effective method for developing your favorite color schemes. Each lesson also presents a set of color and fabric challenges that can be solved while making a wallhanging-size quilt. The projects are simple combinations of squares and triangles which will allow you to concentrate on the colors and fabrics, not the sewing. At the end of each lesson you will find some quilts that have used the basic concept as a springboard to create larger, more complicated designs.

Since these lessons were originally developed as a classroom series, it might be fun for you and a few friends to work on them together. Set aside a couple of hours each week to discuss and begin a project. At the next meeting, the finished quilts can be critiqued and a new lesson started. It's probably a good idea to do the lessons in sequential order, because the information is cumulative.

I know you're going to become deeply involved with each lesson because I've created an atmosphere that will arouse your curiosity and keep you interested. You'll find some fantasy roleplaying techniques and occasionally you will have to rely entirely on the scope of your imagination to resolve a color and fabric problem.

There's just one small disclaimer I feel the need to mention: Don't expect to find step-by-step instructions for making the "Great American Quilt." This is a workbook and these are "learning quilts," not show quilts. The good news is that by the time you are finished, you will own seven terrific little wallhangings and you'll be an expert at putting your favorite colors and fabrics together. Best of all, you will have gained the confidence to start your own version of the "Great American Quilt." And that's a promise!

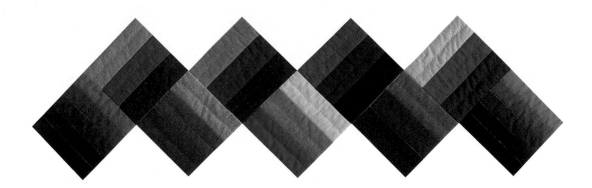

BASIC SUPPLIES

You won't need many gizmos and gadgets to get you through these design lessons, just some simple cutting and sewing tools. Before starting, make sure your equipment is in good working condition. Scissors and rotary cutting blades should be sharp and your sewing machine running smoothly. There's nothing more frustrating than working with ineffective tools; they slow you down and break your concentration. You will need the following items:

- Rotary cutter and cutting mat
- Fabric cutting scissors
- Template plastic
- Transparent acrylic ruler that measures 6" x 24". I also like to have a 2" x 18" transparent acrylic ruler on hand for smaller cutting and measuring tasks.
- Sewing machine and appropriately colored 100% cotton sewing machine thread
- Reducing glass. (When you look at your quilt design through a reducing glass, it gives you the illusion of being at least ten feet away, which makes design flaws more obvious.)
- Flannel-covered design board. (See instructions below.)

Note: Three of the quilt projects require some extra equipment which will be noted at the start of the lesson.

HOW TO MAKE A
FLANNEL-COVERED DESIGN BOARD

A design board allows you to work on a vertical surface, much like an artist working at an easel. Purchase a 40" x 60" piece of foam-core board at a craft or art supply store. These boards come in ¼" and ½" thicknesses. I prefer the ½" thickness. It's a little more expensive, but it's much sturdier. (If you can't find the ½" thickness, the ¼" thickness will do just fine.) Press a 36" x 45" piece of white 100% cotton flannel to remove all the folds and wrin-

kles and then attach it to your foam-core board with straight pins. The board may be leaned against a wall or sturdy chair and you're ready to start designing. The nice thing about working on one of these design boards is that because it's portable, you can move it from room to room. This allows you to examine your quilt top in different kinds of light and from a greater distance.

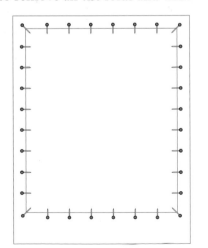

FABRIC PREPARATION

Prewashing fabric is a matter of personal taste and you should follow the dictates of your conscience. Early in my quilting career I made the decision not to wash or even rinse printed fabrics ahead of time. It got to be too much trouble. When I was in the middle of designing a quilt I found it distracting to have to stop and wash the just-purchased fabrics. So now, if I suspect a particular fabric might run, I test it by putting a little snippet in an ounce or two of warm water. If the water changes color, I don't use the fabric. It's that simple. Life is too short to waste time trying to make a fabric colorfast, especially when there are so many other wonderful fabrics to choose from.

When I make a quilt that will be used on a bed, I like to wash it after it has been quilted and bound. Washing a quilt at this point makes it look so crisp and fresh, and it smells so good! I studiously avoid washing wallhanging-size quilts—just a gentle shaking once in awhile to remove dust. I think that when the manufacturer's sizing is left intact, the colors are less likely to fade.

FABRIC QUANTITIES

I have tried to be specific about quantities for each lesson, but when one is designing, and being utterly creative, it's almost impossible to know how much of each fabric will be required. I think you will just have to use some common sense. My rule of thumb is: smaller amounts of more fabrics are better! During the initial design process, I like to buy eighth or quarter yard pieces of all the fabrics I think I might use. If I need more of a particular fabric, I race back to the store. If it's gone, I improvise. That's part of the fun, and also one of the endearing charms of making patchwork.

With the exception of Lesson Seven, wait to buy border and binding fabrics until after the main body of the quilt is designed and sewn. At that point it will be much easier to make an appropriate selection. The amount of fabric needed for binding will depend on your preferred binding method.

READING PREPARATION

I know it's an effort to read all the text in a quilt book. Personally, I spend most of my time looking at the pictures. But please read the Introduction (if you haven't already). It will tell you exactly what you can expect to accomplish by doing the lessons. Also, read the Color and Fabric Notes chapters (beginning on page 9) before starting. You're bound to unearth a few gems of wisdom that will help you along the way. And if you run into any sewing difficulties, you can turn to the Sewing Notes chapter (beginning on page 102) for help.

Each of us sees color with eyes that have been influenced by our cultural heritage, upbringing, and individual preference. Because of this, we carry a built-in bias that dictates how we will respond to any given set of colors. To further complicate the issue, no two people interpret a color in exactly the same way. My idea of a perfect red might be slightly less orange than yours, and I prefer my greens to lean toward blue or yellow.

Some people have the ability to see a broader, more intense spectrum of hues. For them, watching a late afternoon sun paint shimmering rainbows on the walls of the Grand Canyon can be an overwhelming physical experience. For other people, those same awesome moments might be spent looking for a snack bar. Most of us fall somewhere between these two extremes. We are able to appreciate the beauties of nature and the art of our fellow man. When we are designing a quilt and working with colors we love, we feel immensely satisfied. At least we feel satisfied when our selection of fabrics is successfully interpreting our inner vision. When it isn't, we become totally frustrated.

Most of us know when some aspect of our quilt isn't working. The problem is, we don't always know how to fix it. And guess what! It never gets any easier. The more you learn about quilting, the more critical you become of your handiwork and the harder it is to feel satisfied. And this is a good thing because a little dissatisfaction is food for the soul. It will inspire you to try new techniques and increase your knowledge. So, if you're feeling a bit hungry, let's talk about color.

COLOR THEORY BASICS

The first thing you need to know about color is that nothing is constant or absolute! The influence and impact of any given color changes every time it is put into a new environment. Color theory is, at best, a collection of scientific guidelines based on natural laws of harmony and contrast. What does this statement mean? Let me give you an example. Envision a brilliant sunset, with sherbet colors like peach, orange, and raspberry streaking across the sky. If you look at the color circle on page 10, you will find these colors are situated next to each other; they are called analogous. Somewhere along the way color theorists determined that analogous colors should be harmonious (look good together) because they relate directly to familiar events in nature.

I've always felt that it's good to have a working knowledge of color theory, but if you want to make truly artistic quilts that will also reflect your individuality, you should learn to rely on your taste and trust your intuition. With that in mind, I have chosen to highlight just a few important color theory principles. If you would like to learn more about color theory, consult the Bibliography on page 111.

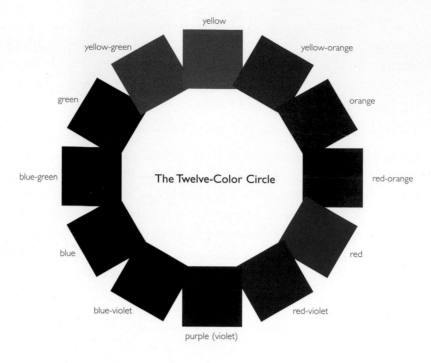

The Twelve-Color Circle

yellow, yellow-green, green, blue-green, blue, blue-violet, purple (violet), red-violet, red, red-orange, orange, yellow-orange

COLOR VOCABULARY

Primary Colors: Red, yellow, and blue. These are the only three colors that can't be created by mixing other colors together.

Secondary Colors: Orange, purple, and green. These colors are made by mixing equal parts of two primary colors. Red + blue = purple. Red + yellow = orange. Yellow + blue = green.

Tertiary Colors: Yellow-orange, red-orange, red-violet, blue-violet, blue-green, and yellow-green. Tertiary colors are created by mixing equal parts of a primary color with a secondary color.

Pure Colors: All the colors on the twelve-color circle are pure colors. They are considered pure because they haven't been diluted with white or darkened with black. A quilt made exclusively with pure colors will be brilliant and powerful, too powerful for many tastes.

Saturated Colors: The intensity of a color. Pure colors are fully saturated. When black or white is added to a color, it becomes less saturated.

Tinted Colors: A mixture of any pure color with white. The more white that is added, the lighter the resulting pastel color will be.

Shaded Colors: A mixture of any pure color with black. The more black that is added, the darker and duller the color will be.

Toned Colors: A mixture of any pure color with gray. The resulting color is mellower than a shade and not as delicate as a tint.

Black and White: Though technically not considered colors, they are frequently used to establish high contrast.

Warm and Cool Colors: The color circle is divided into warm and cool color areas. Reds, yellows, and oranges are warm and have an aura of vitality and energy. They tend to move forward and give the illusion of occupying more space than cool colors. Blues, greens, and purples are cool and transmit feelings of serenity and calm. They will recede and function as backgrounds when combined with warm colors. When designing a quilt, it takes two or three times as much of a cool color to equally balance the impact of a warm color.

Now remember I said earlier that nothing about color is absolute? Here's an example of what I was talking about. In this combination of blue, green, and purple fabric squares, the green (though technically a cool color) performs the function of a warm color and provides a dynamic focus. When the same green squares are put with warm colors, they become the cool element. The lesson to be learned is that the degree of warmth and coolness can be relative and the impact of an individual color should be reassessed each time it is used.

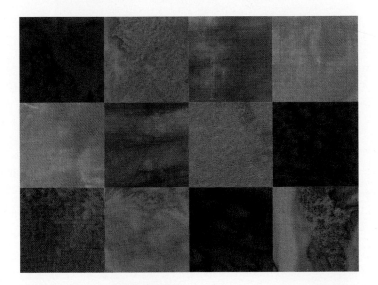

Value: Value relates to the amount of black or white that has been added to a color. A color's value isn't always easy to judge, because in quilting, value is also a relative term. In the following examples, the same red print changes from the light, to the medium, to the dark value. So again, nothing is absolute and the impact of a color must constantly be reevaluated. Lessons Two and Three will give you the opportunity to practice and improve your value assessing skills.

Contrast: The pairing of opposite elements like warm and cool colors or light and dark values. Here is a swatch of red. Because only one color is involved, there can be no contrast (a). When a swatch of blue is added, immediately the *contrast of a warm and a cool color* becomes apparent (b). Adding a pastel tint of green brings *contrast of value* into the mix (c). A grayed shade of purple introduces *contrast of saturation* (d). When the swatches are surrounded with a yellow border print, the *contrast of prints and solids* becomes evident (e). There is also a *contrast of proportion* (large areas opposing smaller areas). As each contrast is added, the combination of colors becomes richer and more interesting. A complete description of the various kinds of contrast useful to quiltmakers can be found at the beginning of Lesson Four (beginning on page 53).

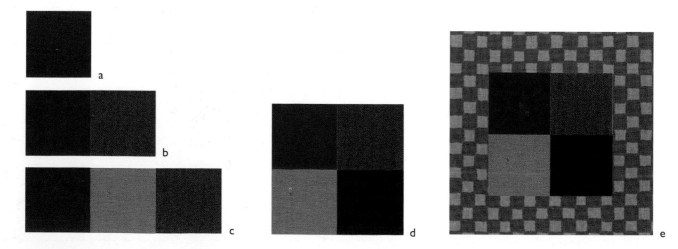

Harmonious Color Schemes: There are five combinations of hues that are generally accepted by theorists to be attractive organizations of color. I've chosen not to go into any detail, beyond simply listing them because there are a *gazillion* other quilt books showing how to interpret these color schemes. In the upcoming lessons you will discover seven more challenging and personalized ways to invent eye-catching color combinations.

- Monochromatic: Tints, tones, and shades of one color.
- Complementary: Colors that appear opposite each other on the color circle.
- Analogous: Three or four colors that are adjacent to each other on the color circle.
- Polychromatic: A combination of warm and cool colors.
- Neutral: Grays, tans, rosy beiges: Almost any color can be put into a neutral color scheme if it's so diluted that it becomes non-competitive.

COLOR FAMILIES

This is where we part company with traditional color theory and use a color system that is more "quilter friendly." Artists have always used a twelve-color circle, like the one pictured on page 10, to help them mix paint. Quilters, on the other hand, have to rely on fabric manufacturers to supply a palette of desirable colors. I'm happy to say the manufacturers do a stellar job, but the point I'm making is this: Because we don't need to physically mix our colors, it makes sense to pare down the twelve-color circle and focus on the six spectrum colors: red, orange, yellow, green, blue, and purple. For each color, we'll create a family of closely related hues, just the way bolts of fabric are most often arranged in quilt shops. In this way, we can become more expansive with our definition of a color. Red, for example, can be anything from the color of a juicy ripe tomato to the ruby luster of a holiday cranberry.

As you work on the lessons, particularly Lesson Two, returning to this page will help you to define and recognize "enriched colors."

Color Families

MAKE A FAVORITE-COLOR SAMPLER

Before starting the lessons, it might be helpful to define (both verbally and visually) your favorite colors. What colors excite you? What colors warm your heart and give you an inner glow when you look at them? As I was writing this chapter, it occurred to me it might be fun to make a little paste-up using tints, tones, and shades of my favorite colors. I was curious to see what they would look like when grouped together.

I started by making a list of my favorite colors: turquoise, watermelon, burgundy, yellow-green, cobalt, and purple. I cut several 1½" squares of these colors from solid fabrics and then used a glue stick to attach the squares to a 8½" x 11" piece of white poster board.

When I looked at the finished sampler, it was glaringly obvious that I like bright colors. Subtlety seems to be missing from my color vocabulary and I'm afraid my paste-up looks like a candidate for a clown suit. This exercise tells me I probably wouldn't want to make a quilt using only my favorite colors, but it does verify my preference for strong contrasts. Perhaps if I had designed this sampler using printed fabrics it might have looked better. As you will learn in the following chapter, the personality of a solid color fabric can be altered and enhanced by the addition of a printed surface. It should be interesting to see what you can learn about your color preference by making a favorite-color sampler of your own.

Favorite-color Sampler

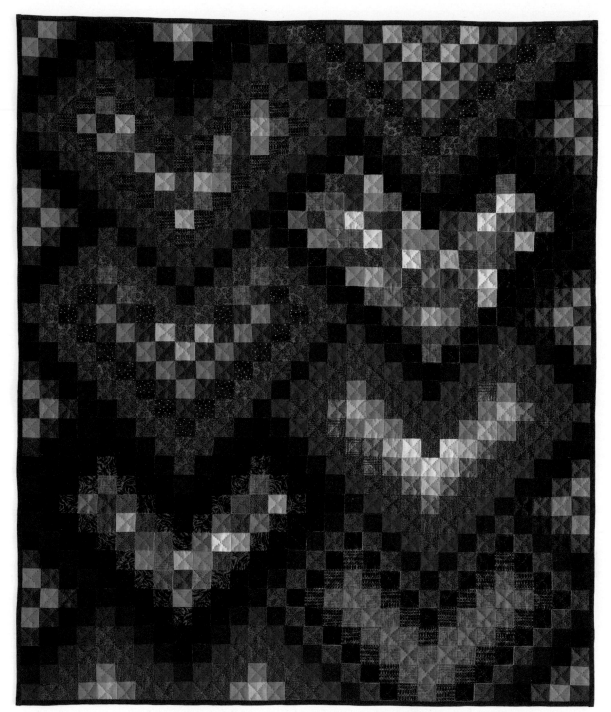

Heart's Delight, Gai Perry, 1998, 38" x 45½" ▲

All the quilts for this book were finished and ready to be photographed when I realized there wasn't an appropriate quilt for the cover. With a name like *Color from the Heart*, how could we use anything but a quilt with hearts on it? I'm not comfortable stitching appliqué, which was the obvious solution, so I sat down with a large piece of graph paper and started doodling. I used the visualization technique described in Lesson Six, and two hours later I had a heart design I was thrilled with. When I thought about translating the drawing in fabrics, I decided to use my favorite-color sampler as a starting point. A diagram for this quilt design can be found on page 109.

A swatch of solid-color fabric is like a paint chip: a simple one-dimensional representation of a color. A group of contrasting solid-color fabrics generally makes a strong graphic statement. A swatch of printed fabric, on the other hand, is more complex. It has a surface personality that renders it unique. A group of printed fabrics can speak volumes. It can shout, whisper, amuse, or enthrall. It can also be very dull!

Our ancestors had it easy when it came to choosing fabrics; they used what was available. Today, when you walk into a quilt store, you are confronted with three hundred years of fabric design. It's no wonder the inexperienced quilter has frequent panic attacks and bouts of insecurity.

With so much fabric at her fingertips, how does a quilter learn to combine a group of prints that will define her personal style and also be consistent with the period and mood she is trying to express? Trial and error would be one method, but wouldn't it be more efficient to be able to recognize the various *surface components* of a printed fabric? Just as the strength of America is built from a melting pot of nationalities and divergent interests, a successfully executed patchwork quilt is the sum of many individual pieces.

SURFACE COMPONENTS

Every printed fabric is defined by five separate surface components. These components are style, pattern, scale, color family, and value.

one: style

The period or temperament of a printed design. There are three major categories shown on the following pages.

Ethnic or Tribal: Prints that suggest a specific culture or geographic location such as China, Africa, India, etc. Ethnic fabrics come in all sorts of delicious flavors. African prints are joyful, displaying bold colors and hard-edge linear movement. Prints with an oriental flair can be resplendent with brilliant colors and touches of shiny gold. Intricate paisleys, with their sinewy curves and rich coloring, have their origins in India.

Traditional: Any printed fabric that looks like it could have been manufactured more than fifty years ago. The colors found on fabrics with patterns borrowed from the eighteenth and nineteenth century are somewhat muted, suggesting a mellow patina that can only be acquired through aging. Prints designed to look as though they were made in the first half of this century favor clear colors and pastel tints.

Contemporary: Bold abstract designs, earthy textures, batiks, and theme oriented prints that depict a recognizable image. Contemporary stripes, plaids, and polka dot prints are more whimsical and less symmetrical than their traditional counterparts. Generally speaking, abstract prints lean toward vivid colors and have strong value contrasts.

two: pattern

The nature of the printed surface design. The pattern helps to define the personality of a fabric. How you choose to combine various patterns (or print personalities) will help to reinforce the mood and time frame of your quilt design. The most eye-catching quilts are created with several different pattern styles.

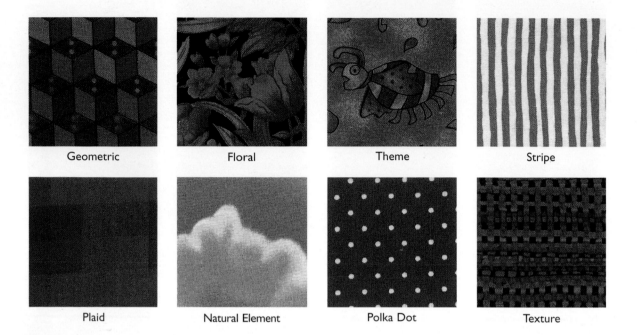

Geometric   Floral   Theme   Stripe

Plaid   Natural Element   Polka Dot   Texture

three: scale

The size of the overall pattern repeat. A quilt made with several different fabrics but just one print scale will lack contrast and definition. All the prints will run together visually and look repetitive and uninteresting. When you select fabrics for a quilt, make a conscious effort to choose a variety of print scales.

  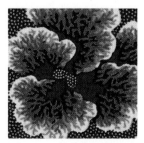 

Small   Medium   Large   Extra Large

four: color family

A tint, tone, or shade of a color that can be identified as one of the six spectrum colors, neutral, multicolored, or black and white. For a more complete description of each color, turn to page 13 in the Color Notes chapter.

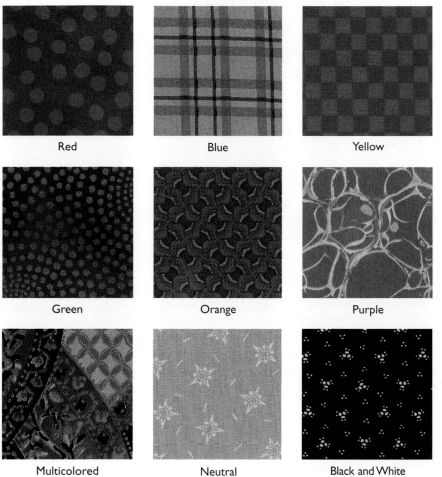

Red	Blue	Yellow
Green	Orange	Purple
Multicolored	Neutral	Black and White

five: value

The amount of white or black that is added to a color to make it appear light, medium, or dark. When a fabric print has a combination of values it can be tricky to categorize. When working with a multicolored combination print, it's hard to determine how the overall value will read until you move a few feet away or look at it through your reducing glass.

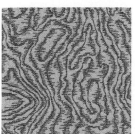

Light	Medium	Dark	Combination

Using the component classification criteria, try to categorize the following swatches of printed fabric.

Fabric A

Style _____

Pattern _____

Scale _____

Color _____

Value _____

Fabric B

Style _____

Pattern _____

Scale _____

Color _____

Value _____

Fabric C

Style _____

Pattern _____

Scale _____

Color _____

Value _____

I hope you are beginning to see that choosing the color palette you want to work with is just the tip of the iceberg. If you were making a traditional quilt and wanted to suggest a feeling of age, it would be wrong to use an obviously contemporary batik or geometric print. Even if the color was absolutely perfect, the newer looking print would skew the authenticity of your design. Frequently, your intuition will tell you when a fabric is inappropriate, but it wouldn't hurt to do some homework. Go to a library, or bookstore, or your local quilt shop and study quilts that appeal to you. Look at the fabrics in the quilts and, using the criteria in this chapter, try to analyze their personalities. It will take time and a little perserverence, but eventually, you should be able to put together some fabrics that express exactly the mood and period you desire.

ANSWERS:
Fabric A - Ethnic style, geometric pattern, medium scale, multicolor, medium value.
Fabric B - Traditional style, textured pattern, medium scale, red color, dark value.
Fabric C - Contemporary style, theme pattern, small scale, neutral color, light value.

Postage Stamp Quilt, Gai Perry, 23" x 26" ▲

O nce upon a time in America, way before how-to books and design classes were available, women somehow managed to make quilts of remarkable beauty and color. Because it was necessary to use tiny leftover scraps and secondhand fabrics, they unknowingly employed two important rules for successfully combining unrelated fabric prints:

rule #1: Most fabrics will blend in a pleasing manner if the size of the individual pattern pieces are small (two inches or less).

rule #2: It is easier to combine fifty different fabrics in a quilt than it is to choose five fabrics that look perfect together.

I have a romantic vision of one of my ancestors sitting by a fire on a cold winter evening. She has a basket of calico squares in her lap and as she tells a bedtime story to her children, she picks up the squares (one at a time) and sews them together. She doesn't agonize over the arrangement of colors; she just methodically stitches the squares into rows, and the rows gradually turn into a dazzling Postage Stamp quilt. This spontaneous method of quilt design is the focus of Lesson One. The results can be even more effective if you work with a group of five or six friends. It's also a congenial way to spend a few hours. You will find instructions for both the individual and group method and no matter which you use, this lesson is going to be fun!

Supplies
- Basic supplies (page 7)
- One lunch-size paper bag
- One shallow basket or container, approximately 9" x 12"
  (This requirement is for the group participation method only.)

FABRICS FOR THE INDIVIDUAL METHOD

Select forty different fabrics. At most, you will need only enough to cut three or four 2" squares from each fabric, so look through your scrap collection before going shopping. Concentrate on prints, but you can also add a few solids. Choose fabrics that are personally appealing and avoid trying to coordinate a color scheme. What you want to end up with is a nice chaotic jumble of colors and patterns. The assortment should include the following:
- Small, medium, and large prints
- Light, medium, and dark values
- A variety of fabric patterns (stripes, plaids, florals, textures, etc.)
- Include at least one yellow and one gold print. Also include a bright red and a dark red, and two turquoise fabrics.

You will need a half yard of an outer border fabric and an eighth yard of an inner border fabric, but wait until the main body of the quilt is complete before making your selections.

Cut three 2" squares from each of the forty fabrics for a total of one hundred and twenty squares. Put all the squares in a lunch-size paper bag and shake it to mix the fabrics.

FABRICS FOR THE GROUP METHOD

Use the criteria for selecting fabrics for the Individual Method, but instead of forty fabrics, each participant will select thirty. Before the group meets, everyone should cut four 2" squares from each of their thirty fabrics. Cut the squares as accurately as possible because you will be sharing half of them with your friends. Each participant will keep two squares from every set of four squares and place them in a lunch-size paper bag. There should be sixty squares in each person's bag. Bring the remaining sixty squares and the "bagged squares" to the group meeting. Also bring your design board. (Note: You might want to make a smaller design board for traveling.)

At the meeting, all participants will put their remaining sixty squares in a shallow communal basket. Seat yourselves around a table and start passing the basket from person to person. With every pass of the basket, each participant will select fifteen squares. (Note: You can look at the squares you are selecting but, to be fair to others, take as short a time as possible.) The basket should go around the circle four times and each person will end up with sixty squares of communal fabric. Participants will add these additional sixty squares to the sixty squares already in their paper bags. Shake the bag to mix the fabrics. The benefit of the Group Method is that each person will be working with a broader range of fabric tastes. Everyone will now proceed to design his or her own individual quilt.

BEGIN THE DESIGN

Stand in front of your design board and without looking, reach into your bag, take out one square, and place it on the upper left-hand corner of the design board. Working from left to right, repeat this process until you have ten squares across the top row. Place the squares, just touching, so no white flannel shows through.

How to begin the design

Following the same procedure, add eleven more rows (ten squares across) for a total of twelve rows. You must practice rigid self-control and put the squares up just as they come out of the bag. No peeking! If you try rearranging the squares at this point, you will defeat the purpose of the exercise. The only reason to exchange a square is when the same fabric appears next to itself.

CRITIQUE

When all one hundred and twenty squares are positioned on your design board, stand a few feet away, or use a reducing glass to critique your Postage Stamp quilt. If you have done this exercise with a group, it would be beneficial to critique each other's work.

Ask the following questions about your design:

- Is there a pleasing balance of colors? Sometimes several closely related hues will be grouped together and you will have to decide whether they make the quilt look awkward-interesting or awkward-unbalanced. Look for happy accidents like colors or prints that until now, you would never dream of putting together—and surprisingly they look good!
- Have you noticed how the red, yellow, and turquoise squares make your quilt sparkle and look lively? Do you think you need to add a few more of them?
- Can you detect a theme to your quilt? Does it look like folk art? Is it traditional, contemporary, or ethnic? Sometimes the style of your quilt will be a candid reflection of your taste in fabrics.
- Do you think you can make the quilt look better?

If you answered yes to the last question, now is the time to make some changes. Do a little rearranging or add some new squares of fabric and delete others. I caution you not to make any more changes than necessary. If you do, the spontaneous charm of the quilt will be lost. Let your intuition tell you when the quilt "feels right."

After I had finished putting the squares for the lesson quilt on my design board, I noticed a folk art color scheme emerging. Because I love these kinds of strong colors, I encouraged the tendency by taking out all the lightest value squares and adding more bright red, purple, and mustard prints.

It doesn't happen often but every once in awhile the resulting quilt looks dull and no amount of rearranging seems to fix it. The first time this happened in class I didn't know what to do, so I suggested to the student that she put all her squares back in the bag and start over. In her second attempt, the quilt looked terrific, and nothing needed to be changed. I was just as surprised as she was.

When you are pleased with the arrangement of squares, it's time to sew your Postage Stamp quilt.

SEWING INSTRUCTIONS

Start by sewing the bottom row of squares together using a ¼" seam allowance. (Refer to my method of sewing straight rows of squares together described on page 103.) Press all the seam allowances in this first row toward the left. Sew the squares together in the row directly above the bottom row and this time, press all the seam allowances to the right. Working toward the top of the quilt, continue sewing rows of squares together and alternate the pressing direction of the seam allowances from row to row. When all the squares are sewn into rows, join the rows. (Note: Pinning at each seam allowance juncture will produce nicely aligned squares and perhaps save some ripping out and resewing.) Press all these seam allowances either up or down. Pressing them in one direction will make the quilt top lay flatter.

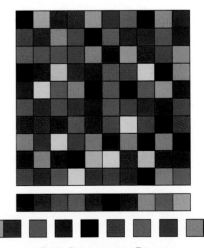

Quilt Construction Diagram

BORDERS

Look at your quilt and decide which two colors you want to emphasize. A general rule of thumb would be to choose a light color fabric (print or solid) for the inner border and a darker or brighter print for the outer border. Cut the inner border strips 1¼" wide. Cut the outer border strips 3½" wide. Attach the borders. Turn to the Sewing Notes chapter starting on page 102, if you need help. If you are a beginning quilter, it would be a good idea to purchase a basic sewing book. Page 111 offers some suggestions. Once the quilt top is assembled, it's ready for quilting. Quilting and finishing instructions begin on page 106.

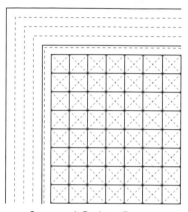

Suggested Quilting Pattern

CONCLUSIONS

Think of this lesson as a warm-up exercise. It s-t-r-e-t-c-h-e-d your fabric tolerance and proved it's possible to put dozens of fabrics and colors into one quilt. The only criterion is that all the pattern pieces must be relatively small. The reasoning is simple: When individual pieces of fabric are cut two inches or less, the eye will accept a kaleidoscope of unrelated, even discordant, colors and prints. When the pattern pieces are larger than two inches the eye tends to look at each fabric individually so one must be more selective when choosing color and print combinations. Imagine what your Postage Stamp quilt would look like if each of the squares measured four or more inches. Not a pretty sight!

Now getting back to Rule #2, which I mentioned at the beginning of this lesson: just keep in mind the adage about "safety in numbers." If you make a quilt with lots of different fabrics, a few less-than-perfect choices will hardly be noticed. From now on, try to incorporate a wider assortment of prints in all your quiltmaking projects. You will be pleased with the results.

The quilts on pages 30–32 show you how to apply this simple paper bag technique to three larger, more imposing designs. And here's an interesting idea: Start cutting a few extra 2" squares from every fabric you use for the next year or so. Put them in a storage container and when several hundred have accumulated, you can start your own heirloom Postage Stamp quilt.

Quilt Gallery

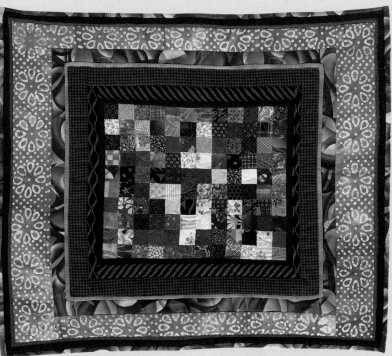

Sharona Fischrup, Piedmont, California ▲

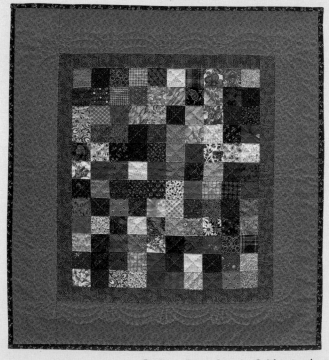

Barbara Beck, Orinda, California ▲

Vivienne Moore, Martinez, California ▲

Two Bag Quilt, Gai Perry, 1997, 47" x 54" ▲

This quilt was a breeze to make because I raided my collection of 2¼" Landscape fabric squares. I put floral prints in one bag, and water and sky prints in a second bag. To design the quilt, all I had to do was pull out squares one at a time, first from one bag and then from the other. When the bags were empty, I stitched the squares together, added borders...and *voilá*, instant quilt!

Straight Furrows Nine-Patch, Gai Perry, 1998, 46" x 58". Machine quilted by June Bell ▲

I used to own an antique shop and early American quilts have always held a special place in my heart. Perhaps this is why I love the challenge of trying to make quilts that look old. A way to guarantee the success of this type of sunshine and shadow effect is to establish a close relationship between the light and dark areas. First, choose light and dark prints from the same color families. Second, put some of the same medium prints in both the light and dark areas. Doing this will form a bond between the light and dark areas and help to promote the illusion of sunshine and shadow. The quilt was made with 1½" (finished size) squares and triangles.

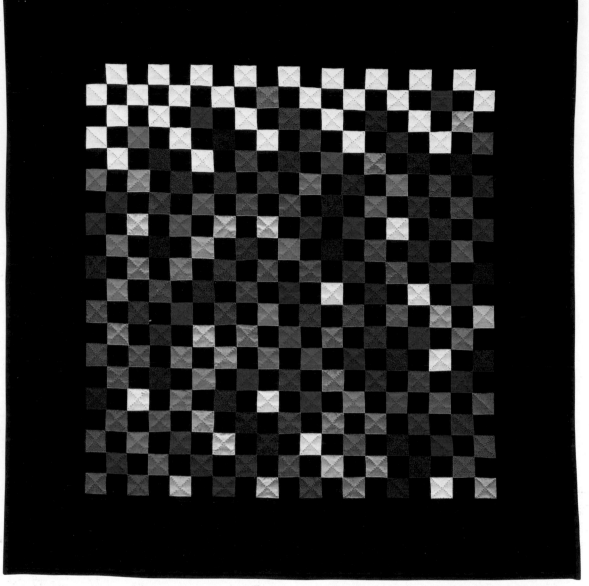

Climbing the Walls, Gai Perry, 1998, 32" x 33¼" ▲

First I established a checkerboard arrangement on my design board with 1¾" black squares. Then I cut what I thought was an equal number of squares from several solid color fabrics. I used hues from every color family except blue. Why did I exclude blue? I don't quite know, but this is where one's intuition kicks in. I guess color selection, like judging values, can also be a "relative thing." On that particular day, the blue shades just didn't feel compatible with the other colors. Maybe on another day I would have excluded the purples.

I put all the colored squares in a paper bag, and this time, I started working at the bottom rather than the top. I hadn't counted correctly so I ran out of colored squares before the design was finished. This turned out to be a happy accident because when I stood back and looked at the quilt, I decided I loved the stark contrast of the black and white rows.

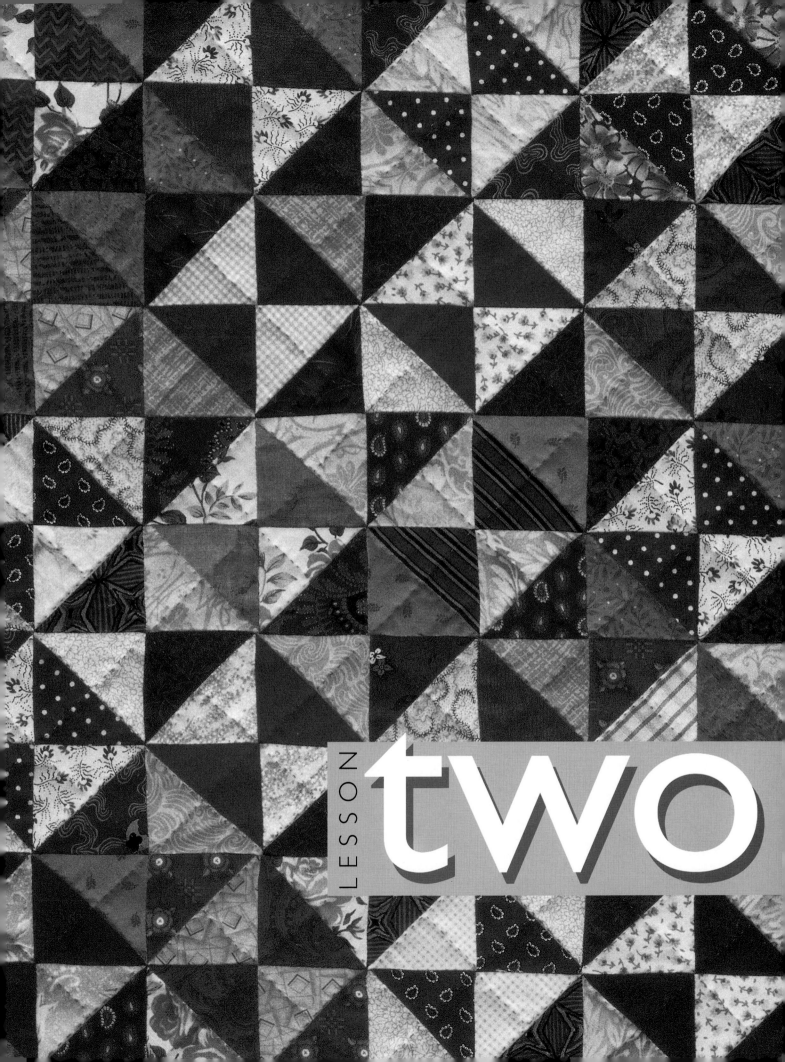

LESSON two

Broken Dishes, Gai Perry, 25" x 29¼" ▲

W hen I was learning how to make quilts, I begged, bought, and borrowed every quilt book I could get my hands on. I'm ashamed to admit I didn't read much of the text, but I spent countless hours studying the photographs. I was particularly attracted to pictures of antique scrap quilts because there seemed to be something so naïve, yet so artful about the way the colors and fabric personalities were blended. I wondered how I could capture this distinctive quality in my own quilts. As I sat thinking about it, a sort of quirky analogy popped into my head. It occurred to me that colors, just like people, have a tendency to thrive when they are supported by a variety of nurturing relationships. We have relatives (a range of tints and shades in the same color group), friends (adjacent colors on the color circle), and lovers (complementary colors that add intensity and sparkle). Yes, I know this concept may sound like a bit of a stretch, but it works for me and it's how I came up with the idea of Color Enrichment.

Color Enrichment is a phrase that describes what occurs when several fabrics with related hues are combined to interpret the essence of a single color.

Look at the photographs of the Broken Dishes quilts that introduce each lesson. I made one for each of the six color families plus one for the neutrals. Notice how each quilt pushes the color range within its own group. The red quilt, on page 67, has a predominance of true red fabrics, but it also has some reds that lean toward orange and red-violet. I've even inserted a few of the fabrics that appear in the orange quilt (on page 33) to show you how the influence of a color can be manipulated. In the red quilt, they look red; in the orange quilt, they appear orange. Now study the quilt for this lesson. You will find that it contains every color in the rainbow, but it still projects the feeling of a pink and green color scheme. The whole point of Color Enrichment is to add as many colors as possible without changing the integrity of the original color scheme.

Supplies
■ Basic supplies only (page 7)

THE FABRICS

Choose two main colors. Plan on using scraps of approximately thirty fabrics, equally divided between the two colors. (Note: A few fabrics more or less won't make any difference.) It would be easier to work with a warm-cool combination like blue and orange, but you can choose any two of your favorite colors. The lesson quilt on page 34 uses pink (which is a tint of red) and its green complement. If you prefer to work with either warm or cool colors exclusively, that's fine, too.

To give you an idea of how to choose fabrics, we'll use my lesson quilt as an example. Before shopping, I went through my fabric collection looking for a family of pink prints in a range that included red-orange through red-violet. I also looked for green prints ranging from blue-green through yellow-green. (Going back to my analogy, these prints would be relative colors.) Then I branched out and added pink and green combination prints having subtle amounts of other colors in them, too (the friendship colors). Since pink and green are complements, the love interest is built in, but if you were making a green and blue quilt, like the one shown on page 42, you would want to add subtle amounts of red and orange (the complements of green and blue) to make the sparks fly. If you need to purchase additional fabrics for this lesson, don't get more than eighth yard cuts.

The quilt block you're going to work with is called Broken Dishes. There is just one size of triangle involved and, as you can see by looking at the block diagram, it contains four different fabrics (each fabric is used twice) and four distinct values: light, medium-light, medium-dark, and dark. As I gathered fabrics, I was careful to select a variety of print patterns and scales. You've probably noticed that the fabrics in my pink and green lesson quilt are also consistently traditional in nature. You may want to try for a more contemporary or ethnic look.

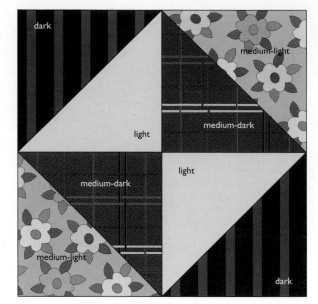

Broken Dishes Block

Divide your selected fabrics (co-mingling both colors) into four value piles: light, medium-light, medium-dark, and dark. (This is the most difficult part of the lesson because the ability to recognize comparative values takes lots of practice.) When you have finished sorting, I'm sure you will notice that most of your fabrics are in the medium-light and medium-dark piles. Eighty percent of the fabrics we buy fall into the medium value category. Who knows why! Maybe medium values are less threatening. You will probably need to purchase some additional light and dark prints.

BEGIN THE DESIGN

To design the first block, choose one fabric from each of the four value piles. Think of the block as a complete miniature quilt and focus on combining a contrast of color, print scale, and pattern. Refer to the Fabric Notes section (beginning on page 16) if you need help.

Note: When working with triangles, sew a straight-grain edge to a bias edge wherever possible. Sewing triangles this way prevents stretching. The straight grain stabilizes the bias.

Method for Cutting Opposing-Grain Triangles

Cut one 3" square from the light fabric.
Then cut in half diagonally.
Cut one 3" square from the medium-light fabric.
Then cut in half diagonally.
Cut one 4¼" square from the medium-dark fabric.
Then cut in half diagonally twice.
Cut one 4¼" square from the dark fabric.
Then cut in half diagonally twice.

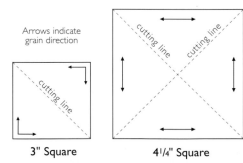

Arrows indicate grain direction

3" Square   4¹/4" Square

Arrange eight of the appropriate value triangles on the upper left corner of your design board. Refer to the Broken Dishes block, on page 36, for the correct placement. When this is done, critique your first block. Can you see four distinct values? Are both of your colors represented? Do you see a nice contrast of print and pattern scale? If you answered no to any of the above questions, select and cut some substitute fabrics.

Here are two examples of the Broken Dishes block. Both blocks have four different value fabrics, but the block on the right also has a nice contrast of pattern and print scale, making it the more desirable example.

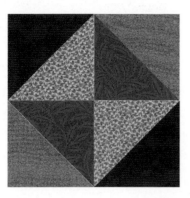 

Design another block and place it directly to the right of the first block. Try to place the triangles just touching, so no white flannel shows through. This will enable you to see the interaction of the colors from one block to another.

IMPORTANT! Individual fabrics may be repeated, but to ensure that you incorporate as many colors and patterns as possible, please try not to use the same fabric in more than three blocks.

Continue designing blocks until there are four complete blocks on the top row. Then continue to design blocks until you have completed five rows. (Four blocks in each row for a total of twenty blocks.) You will probably design at least six blocks before you begin to get a feel for what you are doing. At this point you may want to improve the first few blocks by making them look less tentative; more lively. Interesting to note: When combining a warm and a cool color of seemingly equal value, the cool color will always appear darker when viewed from a distance.

CRITIQUE

When all twenty blocks are positioned on the design board, stand back a few feet and ask these questions:
- Is the two-color scheme recognizable?
- Is there enough color variation to see the benefit of this Color Enrichment technique?
- Is there a pleasing variety of print scales and fabric patterns?
- Can you see an overall contrast of values?
- Is there enough contrast to make the quilt look interesting?

When you can answer yes to all these questions, the quilt is ready to be sewn. Before you start, double check each block to make sure all the values are in the proper order. It's easy to juxtapose a value position without noticing it.

SEWING INSTRUCTIONS

I found it was easier to sew the quilt in rows rather than blocks. Start with the bottom row and sew the pairs of triangles into eight squares. Press all the seam allowances toward the darker triangle and clip off the points. (Refer to the Sewing Notes starting on page 102 if you don't know the "how and why" of clipping points.) Sew the eight squares together and press all the seam allowances toward the left. Continue sewing rows in this manner, alternating the pressing direction of each row.

When all the rows of squares are sewn, check for placement errors and join the rows. Choose a pressing direction and press all the seam allowances either up or down.

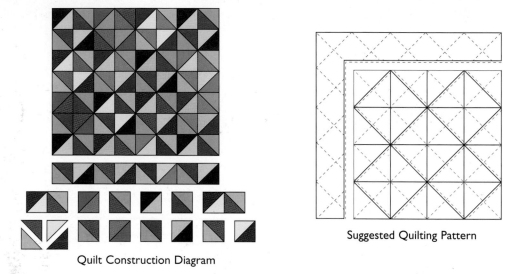

Quilt Construction Diagram

Suggested Quilting Pattern

BORDERS

You will need a half yard of fabric for the outer border and a quarter yard for the inner border. Obviously, you will want to emphasize the *enriched* color scheme by choosing prints in those two colors. Cut the inner border strips 1¼" wide. Cut the outer border strips 3½" wide. Attach the borders. See page 104–105 for help. Quilt and finish as desired, using the instructions beginning on page 106 for guidance.

CONCLUSIONS

The concept of Color Enrichment is the most important lesson in this book and its principle can be applied to every quilt you make. Whether you are using a single color or several, just remember to include a range of tints, tones, and shades for each hue in the chosen color scheme. The finished piece will have an added richness and depth, particularly when compared to a similar style quilt with color families having a limited range of hues.

Quilt Gallery

Vivienne Moore, Martinez, California ▲

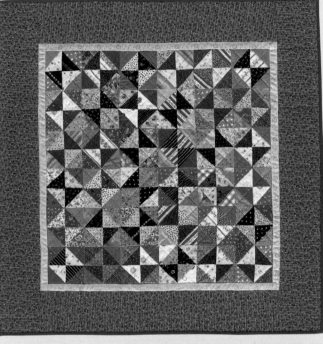

Josephine Jarvis, Oakland, California ▲

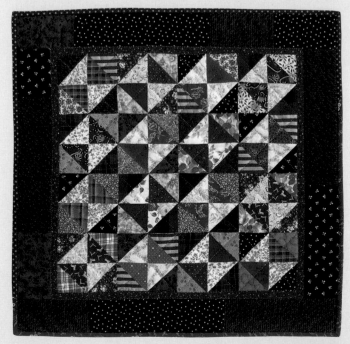

Andrea Carlin, Walnut Creek, California ▲

Lee Fowler, Walnut Creek, California ▲

Peaches and Pansies, Gai Perry, 1998, 48" x 57" ▲

Individually, my favorite colors remain constant, but my attraction to certain color combinations tends to change from one year to the next. Purple and peach is one of my favorite color combinations right now. Another is purple with shades of yellow-green and blue-green. Do your color preferences keep changing, and do you reflect the changes in your quiltmaking?

This color-enriched *Peaches and Pansies* quilt looks very romantic to me. It belongs in a bedroom with scented sheets and frilly lingerie. The block couldn't be simpler: two dark and two light (4" finished size) triangles set on point. The pansy block that is appliquéd to the lower right corner was a last minute whim.

Country Cousins, Gai Perry, 1987, 51" x 61" ▲

This is a comfort quilt. The mellow colors are soothing and make me think of country antiques and summers on a farm. I chose an assortment of traditional-looking plaids and textures. The gold color moves all the way to brown, and the blue from blue-white to blue-black. It's interesting to notice how some of the plaids create a feeling of transparency. I can't take credit for this phenomenon; it just happened. The quilt block is called Corn and Beans.

Kaleidoscope, Gai Perry, 1998, 40" x 46" ▲

I combined contemporary prints from the blue and green color families to make this 1990s version of the Kaleidoscope pattern. The Enrichment technique is evident in colors ranging from lime through blue-violet. Looking at this quilt, I can see that I intuitively ignored the medium value fabrics in order to get a stronger contrast between the light and dark prints.

Notice that I added three obvious touches of red (the complement of green) to give the quilt even more intensity. The red is strategically placed to form an irregular triangle. I've learned that if one takes the lightest or brightest color and arranges it in a triangular pattern, it helps to lead the viewer's eye around the surface of the quilt.

LESSON three

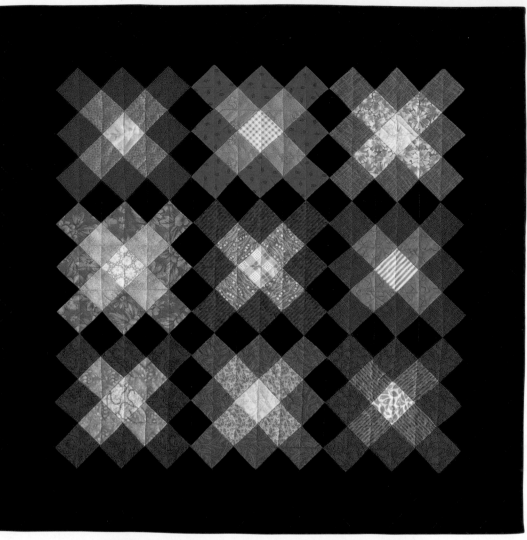

Dark-to-Light Value Arrangement, Gai Perry, 24$^{1}/_{2}$" × 24$^{1}/_{2}$". Machine Quilted by June Bell ▲

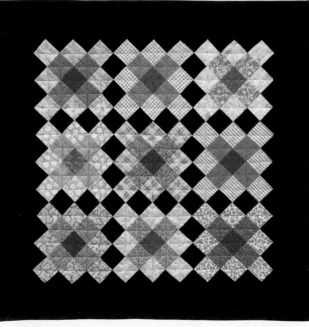

Light-to-Dark Value Arrangement, Gai Perry, 24$^{1}/_{2}$" × 24$^{1}/_{2}$" ▲
Machine Quilted by June Bell

I f you've been on this planet for fifty years or more, or ever watched the "Roseanne" show, you are probably aware of the crocheted wool afghans our grandmothers used to make. With love and unwavering determination, they would make one for each member of the family. If you browse through antique shops and flea markets you are sure to find countless examples of these practically indestructible throws.

Afghans contain dozens of colorful squares that are framed by rows of horizontal and vertical sashing. Black was frequently used as a background color for fabric projects in the 1930s and 1940s. Women's magazines suggested it was the perfect choice to accent the flour sack prints that were popular during that period.

Individual blocks in an afghan usually contain three or four values of one or two colors. Sometimes the values were arranged light-to-dark, and other times, dark-to-light. The most vivid afghans have a combination of both. I admit to having a love-hate attraction to these old throws and I think their arrangement of squares is an effective way to work on value recognition.

Supplies
■ Basic supplies only (page 7)

THE FABRICS

When you study the lesson quilt examples, you will notice that because I was trying to retain the flavor of the old afghans, I used fabrics that are reminiscent of that era: small-scale floral prints, ginghams, and ice cream colored pastels. These kinds of fabrics are being reproduced today, so you shouldn't have any trouble finding them at your local quilt shop.

I've worked the lesson two ways: dark-to-light values against black, and light-to-dark values, also against black. Choose the example you like best and use it as your design reference. If you prefer a softer look, you could use unbleached muslin or a creamy tone-on-tone print for the background fabric.

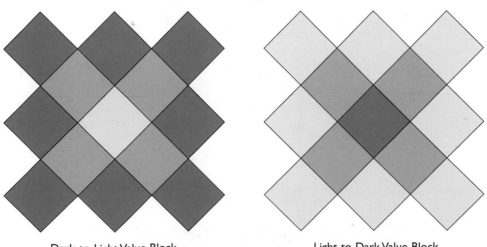

Dark-to-Light Value Block   Light-to-Dark Value Block

First go through your fabric collection, then if you need to purchase additional fabric, buy eighth yard cuts of the colored fabrics and one yard of the background fabric.

Try to find prints in a light, medium, and dark value run for nine different colors. If you choose a red-orange color, make sure the particular shade of red-orange is consistent in all three values. Also, and this is the hard part, *try to get the light, medium, and dark values in each color range to be equal.* Look at the value run examples. This was how I organized my fabrics to see if the values were consistent in each color range. I kept substituting swatches until I thought I'd done the best possible job with what was available. You can use any combination of prints and solids and always consider using the reverse side of a fabric. It might be just the shade you're looking for.

Don't expect perfection in all your value runs. Even professionally-dyed value runs can have flaws. Allow one week to gather fabrics. Try swapping with friends. At the end of the week, select the value run in each color that you think will work the best. If you can't put nine acceptable value runs together, work with six and make a smaller, rectangular quilt.

▶ After a week of searching and substituting, these are the fabrics I decided to use. Two of the prints are shown on the reverse side because I needed the color to appear just a little bit lighter. Between the time I made this paste-up and put the quilts together, I came across a medium value orange print that I thought was just slightly better.

Value Run Examples

BEGIN THE DESIGN

Cut the appropriate number of 2" colored squares for the first block and place them on the upper left-hand corner of your design board. Refer to the block diagram of your choice for the correct arrangement and square count. Continue designing blocks and use the lesson quilts (on page 44) as your guide for the placement of the blocks. Notice that I used four cool color value runs and five warm color value runs and I arranged the blocks in a warm-cool alternating sequence. You may decide to arrange the blocks differently.

When all the colored squares are in place on your design board, cut twenty-eight 2" black squares (or whatever light background color you might be using) and put them in the blank spaces between the blocks. Helpful hint: If you are using black for the background, choose the darkest black fabric you can find; it will provide the best contrast with the colored squares.

From the same background fabric, cut eight 3⅜" squares and cut each square diagonally twice, into four triangles. Place them around the perimeter. Cut two 2" squares and cut each square diagonally, into two triangles. Put one at each corner. Refer to the triangle cutting instructions shown below.

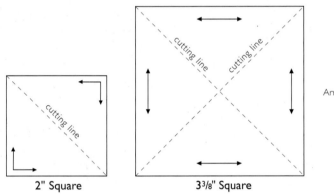

2" Square   3³/₈" Square

Arrows indicate grain direction

CRITIQUE

Stand back from your design board. If you have an instant or digital camera, take a picture of your quilt. It will help to determine if there are three distinct values in each block. Also use your reducing glass. Ask yourself the following questions:

- Do all the dark prints look equally dark in value?
- Do the mediums and lights look equal in value? If not, you might give it one more try. It seems contradictory, but sometimes a fabric that's not the most perfect choice will look better when it's cut into squares and put into the block; possibly because the print is more interesting or the color is truer when viewed from a distance.

When you've done the best you can, don't look back—sew it!

Surprisingly, some of the best examples I've seen of this lesson are quilts with flawed value runs but for some reason (perhaps the charm of the individual fabrics) the overall effect is full of personality and character.

SEWING INSTRUCTIONS

This quilt will first be sewn into diagonal rows and then the rows will be stitched together. Start in the lower left corner and sew the square to its two perimeter triangles. Press all the seam allowances in this first row toward the left. Sew the second diagonal row of squares and perimeter triangles together and press all the seam allowances toward the right. Note: My method for joining straight rows of squares (page 103) works equally well with these diagonal rows. Continue sewing rows and alternate the pressing direction of the seam allowances. When all the rows are sewn, join them together. Choose a pressing direction and press all the seam allowances either up or down.

Quilt Construction Diagram

BORDERS

I didn't think it would be appropriate to use a different or contrasting fabric for the borders on these lesson quilts. I was concerned that whatever color I chose would skew the balance of the nine value runs. But I was wrong! The student quilts, on page 49, show considerably more thought and creativity.

The border strips for the lesson quilts were cut 3" wide. Quilt and finish as desired.

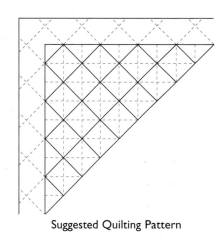

Suggested Quilting Pattern

CONCLUSIONS

I've learned that one of the most difficult things a quilter has to do is to decide on the comparative value of a group of fabrics. Which is the lightest, which is the darkest? The rule to remember is this: *The value of a fabric is relative to what is put next to it.* A particular fabric may be the darkest value in one block and change to the middle value in the block right next to it. Each time you use a particular fabric, its value has to be reexamined.

I've always found it helpful to squint my eyes when I'm trying to decide on the comparative value of two fabrics. But try using a reducing glass. It's a better option, and it won't encourage wrinkles.

Quilt Gallery

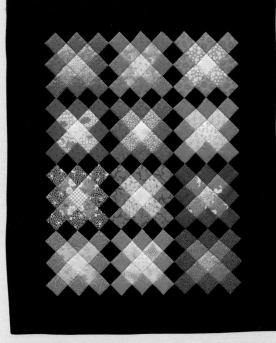

Lee Fowler, Walnut Creek, California ▲

Andrea Carlin, Walnut Creek, California ▲

Vivienne Moore, Martinez, California ▲

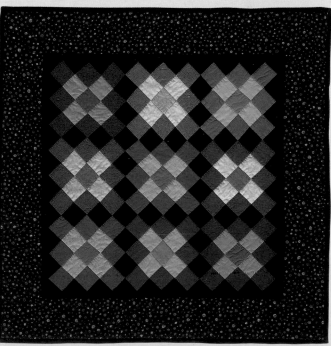

Catherine Comyns, Pleasant Hill, California ▲

Great Granny Squares, Gai Perry, 1990, 56" x 61" ▲

It was inevitable that one day I would make this quilt. Ever since I used the pattern to teach my value recognition lesson, I'd been obsessing over the need to make an afghan-style quilt. Great Granny Squares is a compilation of every afghan I've ever seen. Some of the blocks have only one color; some have two. Still others have one color plus black. The only consistency is the movement in each block from light to dark.

Diamonds and Squares, Gai Perry, 1985, 51" x 51" ▲

I switched from squares to triangles to make this value-graded quilt. The composition and placement of the light-to-dark triangles makes the quilt appear to shimmer with reflected light. The graphic image feels contemporary, but the use of traditional fabrics reinforces the origin of this nineteenth-century pattern.

The block I used is called a Split Nine-Patch. Each of the squares is split in half and value-graded: lightest value in the lower right corner to darkest value in the upper left corner. Each split square must also have a lighter and a darker triangle. This would be a great quilt on which to practice your value recognition skills. It's best to design four blocks at a time; every four blocks complete one of the nine light-to-dark diamonds on point.

Family Values, Gai Perry, 1998, 50" x 58". Machine quilted by June Bell ▲

I was given a set of tiny swatches that were samples from a collection of hand dyed, value-graded fabrics. They sat around gathering dust for a couple of years until I figured out how to use them. First I stitched each color range into a 6" square. Then I set the squares on point and alternated the placement of the warm and cool colors. This design would look fabulous if it was made with warm and cool value-graded prints instead of solids.

Primary Colors, Gai Perry, 23" x 30" ▲

The most vivid recollection I have of kindergarten is my "Princess and the Castle" series. I spent the entire year drawing the same picture over and over again. And when the drawing was finished, I had a precise coloring ritual that never wavered. I began by filling in the castle walls with a bright yellow crayon. Then I would go over the yellow with a red crayon and then again with a blue crayon. The result was a multicolor glaze which, to my young eyes, was truly magical. The princess always had yellow hair, a long blue dress, and red shoes.

These early efforts are perfect examples of how children and primitive artists repeatedly choose to work with the primary triad of red, yellow, and blue. As a child grows, or an artist is trained, their color choices become more complex. Do you remember your first quilt efforts? Were they simple variations of the primary triad? Mine were. Then gradually as I took classes and made more quilts, my palette expanded and I was able to put all kinds of seemingly unrelated colors and fabrics together.

Primitive artists and children love working with the primary triad because the vibrant colors and strong contrasts demand instant attention. As adults, we generally try to be more subtle in our pursuit of recognition, but whether you are a novice quilter or an accomplished one, you need to understand that the effective use of contrast can often turn an ordinary design into an extraordinary one.

There are several ways to put more contrast in your quilts. The following types of contrasts are easy to understand and wonderfully adaptable to quiltmaking.

Contrast of Color

Black and white represent the extreme expression of dark and light contrast. Their counterpart, the primary triad of red, yellow, and blue, represents the most extreme expression of color contrast. Another effective, though slightly less brilliant, example of color contrast is the secondary triad of orange, purple, and green. To be assured of color contrast in your quilt design, choose some colors that are three or more spaces apart on the color circle. For the ultimate contrast of color, try combining one brilliant color with black and white. An example of this contrast is shown on page 62.

Contrast of Warm and Cool Colors

This contrast is the one most widely used by artists and quilters. All it requires is that colors are used from both the warm and cool sides of the color circle.

Contrast of Value

This contrast is achieved with a selection of fabrics having a variety of light, medium, and dark values. If you want to put an even stronger value contrast into a quilt, eliminate most of the medium values and emphasize the darks and lights. You can find an example of this contrast on page 63. Many quilters seem to ignore or forget value contrast and design quilts with a predominance of medium values. When this happens, individual colors lack definition and all the elements in the quilt seem to run together.

Contrast of Complementary Colors

Complementary colors sit directly opposite each other on the color circle. When they are used together, they enhance each other's best attributes. The combination of yellow, the most brilliant color, and purple, the darkest color on the color circle, is the most extreme example of complementary contrast. The nice thing about complementary contrast is that it offers the built-in contrast of warm and cool colors. The pink and green Broken Dishes lesson quilt on page 34 illustrates this contrast.

Contrast of Saturation

This is the contrast between intensely bright colors and colors that have been darkened with black or gray. Many early Amish quilts contain glowing examples of this contrast. *Fans and Crazy Patch* on page 64 is a good example of contrast of saturation.

Contrast of Fabric Personality

Combining fabrics with a variety of print scales and patterns creates contrast of fabric personality. Most of the quilts in this book have this contrast. The only exceptions are those made with solid colors.

Contrast of Quilting Design

Occasionally, just for a change of pace, I try to include curves and circles somewhere in the quilting pattern. I find the contrast of the hard-edge patchwork shapes with the circular stitching very satisfying. Examples of this type of contrast can be found on pages 65 and 75.

For this lesson, I'm going to ask you to make a quilt using the primary triad of red, yellow, and blue. Yes, I know I'm asking a lot! Who wants to make a quilt using crayon colors? But the benefits will outweigh the drawbacks because you get to practice working with a controlled palette of colors and fabric personalities. Also, if you have never designed a quilt with premeditated contrasts, this is a good opportunity.

You will be making six Cake Stand blocks. They will be set on point with alternate squares and triangles of fabric acting as the background. Before you begin, decide whether you are going to design a traditional, contemporary, or ethnic style quilt and choose your fabrics accordingly. Look at pages 17–19 if you need to refresh your memory on the definitions of these styles. Try to think like a primitive artist and focus on strong contrasts and bright colors.

Supplies
- Basic supplies (page 7)
- Glue stick
- Template plastic
- 8½" x 11" piece of white paper

THE FABRICS

Assemble an assortment of red, yellow, and blue prints. Remember to enrich the palette with various tints, tones, and shades of these three colors. You may also add the two non-colors, black and white. The lesson example on page 54 uses twelve stylized florals, solids, and contemporary prints. You will notice touches of green in the border fabric. I broke my own rule here but I fell in love with the silly oversize flowers, so I invoked what is called "artistic license." This is a vague term that helps to justify bending the rules.

Homespuns, checks, pillow ticking, and plaids are excellent choices if you are planning to make a traditional style quilt. If you're searching for an idea, why not take this opportunity to make a patriotic Fourth of July wallhanging.

Because the design will be an experiment for you, it is impossible to predict how much fabric you will need. If you don't own any red, yellow, and blue prints, buy some eighth yard cuts for starters. You can always purchase more later. One nice thing about buying small amounts of lots of fabrics is that it quickly builds up your collection of scraps. Scraps make the most interesting quilts because, out of necessity, you are forced to use a greater variety of fabric personalities.

You will choose the fabric or fabrics for the alternate blocks after the Cake Stand blocks are pieced. This way you can lay your blocks on the potential alternate block fabrics (either at home or in the quilt shop) to see which ones look the best.

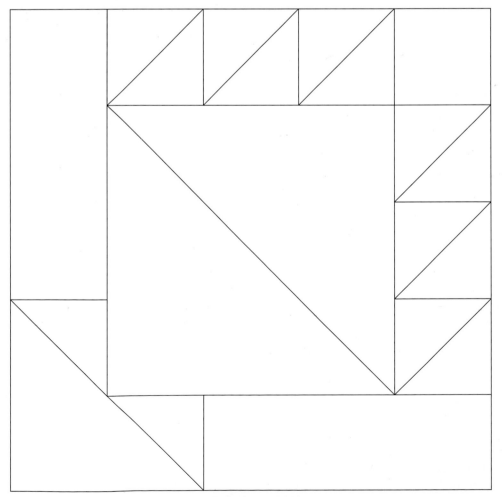

5" Cake Stand Block

BEGIN THE DESIGN

Trace or photocopy the Cake Stand block (page 57) onto a piece of white paper. Now you are going to make a paste-up of the block using your selected fabrics.

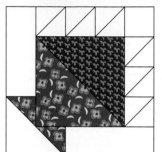

step 1 Start by picking a print for the large lower triangle and the two small triangles at the base of the cake stand. Rough-cut the triangles to the approximate size and place them on the paper pattern. (Note: I suggest rough-cutting because it's quicker. My philosophy is: I'm either going to make a perfect paste-up or a perfectly sewn block; not both.)

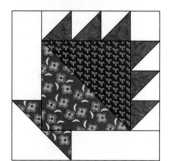

step 2 Now choose a print or solid for the large top triangle and repeat the rough-cutting process. Place it on the paper pattern.

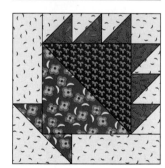

step 3 Decide what fabric or fabrics you want to use for the cake stand points and rough-cut six triangles. Place them on the paper pattern.

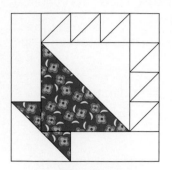

step 4 Finally, pick the background print or prints and rough-cut the six smaller triangles, one square, two rectangles, and the larger triangle. Place them on the pattern.

If you like the way the block looks, use a glue stick to secure the fabrics to the paper pattern. With paper scissors, cut around the perimeter of the paste-up and pin it to your design board. Stand back and decide whether the contrasts hold up from a distance. If you don't like what you see, make some changes. When the paste-up is satisfactory, you can cut the actual pattern pieces using the templates found on page 110. Sew the first block together using the block construction diagram as a guide. Note: When you are making scrappy looking blocks with many different fabrics, it is quicker, more efficient, and less wasteful to use templates. This exercise will also give you the opportunity to practice working with templates if you've never tried using them before.

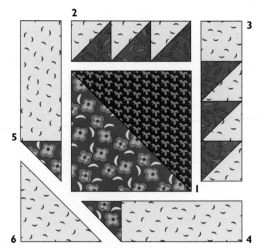

Block Construction Diagram

Now you must decide whether all six blocks are going to be the same or if each one will be different. Look at the lesson example and the student quilts for ideas. Have some fun with these blocks. Perhaps each one of the cake stand points could be a different fabric. Let your imagination run wild! Just remember to concentrate on using fabrics that are suitable to the style you have chosen. I don't think it will be necessary to make any more paste-ups (unless you want to). Go ahead and design the remaining five blocks on your design board using actual-size pattern pieces. When they look the way you want them to, sew the blocks together and put them back on your design board in their correct position. Refer to the lesson quilt for the proper arrangement.

Determine which fabric or fabrics you want to use for the alternate squares and triangles. Cut two 5½" squares for the alternate center squares. Cut two 8⅜" squares and then cut them diagonally (twice) into four triangles. These will be the perimeter triangles. (Note: There will be two triangles left over. If this seems wasteful to you, use the triangle template provided on page 110.) Cut two 4⅜" squares and cut them in half diagonally for the four corner triangles. If you choose a stripe or a directional print, think about the orientation of the lines before cutting the fabric. Position the squares and triangles on your design board. When you are pleased with the overall design of your quilt, sew it together.

SEWING INSTRUCTIONS

You will start by sewing the rows into diagonal strips, just as you did in Lesson Three. Begin at the lower left-hand corner and sew the two perimeter triangles to the block. Press all the seam allowances in this first strip toward the left. Sew the next diagonal strip together and press all the seam allowances toward the right. Continue sewing diagonal strips and alternate the pressing direction. When all the strips are sewn, join them together. Choose a pressing direction and press all the seam allowances either up or down. Refer to the quilt construction diagram.

Quilt Construction Diagram

BORDERS

How many? How wide? How much fabric? The choice is yours. Look at the examples on page 61 for inspiration. Remember that the character of the border fabrics should be consistent with the rest of the quilt. If you want to emulate the border on the lesson example, cut 1" wide strips for the inner border, 1¼" wide strips for the middle border, and 3½" wide strips for the outer border. No matter how many border strips you plan to put around your quilt top, the method for attaching them is always the same. (See instructions beginning on page 104.) Quilt and finish as desired.

CRITIQUE

Ask these questions about your finished quilt:

■ Is there a strong contrast of colors?
■ Is there an obvious contrast of values?
■ Is there an exciting mixture of print pattern and scale?
■ Is the style of fabrics consistent with the theme you selected?

If you have answered yes to all four questions, give yourself an A for Lesson Four.

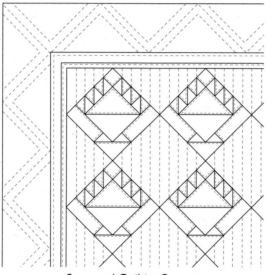

Suggested Quilting Pattern

CONCLUSIONS

This probably isn't a quilt you would want to make every day but the experience you've gained by working with a controlled palette of brightly contrasting colors should help you with future designs. Some day, when the quilt you are working on seems a little bland and uninteresting, you will know why. And then you will find a way to add more contrast.

Quilt Gallery

Trish Katz, Antioch, California ▲

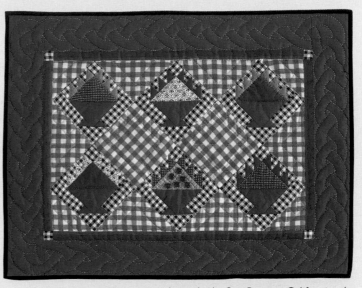

Joyce Lytle, San Ramon, California ▲

Verna Mosquera, Dublin, California ▲

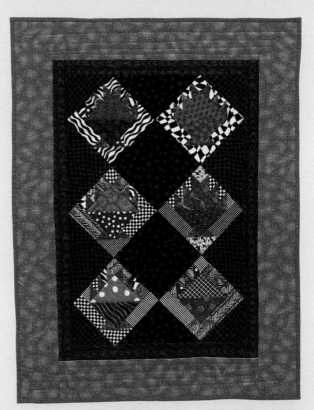

Laurel Samberg, Walnut Creek, California ▲

Navajo, Gai Perry, 1987, 29" x 41" ▲

Several years ago I visited Santa Fe. I was hoping to be inspired by a palette of soft desert colors, but came home with visions of Navajo blankets dancing in my head. The use of black and white, combined with the most vibrant red I could find, produced a quilt containing the ultimate contrast of color.

Leftovers, Gai Perry, 1987, 51" x 61" ▲

I had just finished making a quilt with a very controlled palette of colors and contrasts, and many of the unused fabrics were still littering my sewing room floor. I decided to put them all in this quilt. The predominant use of light and dark prints gives the quilt a crisp hard-edge appearance. I researched the origin and name of the block, but couldn't find any information.

Fans and Crazy Patch, Gai Perry, 1989, 32" x 32" ▲

Here is is a perfect example of contrast of saturation. The dark, grayed tones of the crazy patch squares make the hot pink and red-orange fabrics practically leap off the surface of the quilt.

Study In Contrast, Gai Perry, 1989, 55" x 55" ▲

This quilt is a conscious attempt to orchestrate a design with exaggerated contrasts and balances. Every element has a counter balance to support the movement of color across the surface of the quilt.

For the central block, I chose a brilliant solid red fabric and paired it with a dark print for the contrasts of saturation and fabric style. Two other contrasts working in this section are the contrasts of value and warm-cool colors. The quilt has three light gray borders that get progressively wider as they move toward the outer edge, giving the quilt a nice sense of growing proportion. I put a bright red border between two of these cool gray borders to establish a back and forth rhythm of warm-cool colors. There is also a border composed of warm and cool prints and solids that, as a whole, read as a medium value area. This section was put here to give the viewer's eye a rest.

Finally, since every element of the quilt is made up of sharp points and linear movement, I used a quilting pattern of overlapping circles and cables to give the quilt a final contrast of straight lines opposing curves.

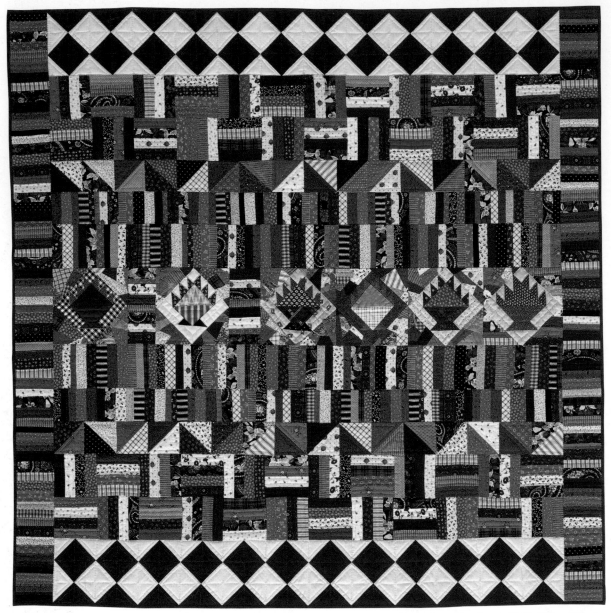

Serendipity, Gai Perry, 1990, 55" x 55" ▲

Serendipity means happening on fortunate discoveries when not looking for them. This quilt is the result of three such circumstances. The string pieced sections were inspired by a photograph in one of my quilt books. The idea for the diamond-on-point border was borrowed from a scrap quilt owned by a friend, and the Cake Stand blocks were made for me by some of my students.

Although this folk art style quilt was made with a predominately red, yellow, and blue color scheme, it has been enriched with several touches of green. I like to think of green as a fourth primary color.

LESSON five

Phoenix, Gai Perry, 33" x 33". Machine quilted by June Bell ▲

Orchestrating a beautiful arrangement of colors without using a visual reference can be difficult. Early in my quilting career, most of my inspiration came from books. I copied my little heart out and it never occurred to me to try anything original. Then one day I was browsing through an issue of *Architectural Digest* and I came across a photograph of a lovely oriental screen. It was painted with such a mellow combination of warm and cool color tones that it quite took my breath away. I was inspired! I bought a piece of 8 x 8 graph paper and started composing an original design. It turned out to be a simple arrangement of light-to-dark value solid color fabrics but the combined hues were true to the picture of the antique screen and I was quite happy with the finished quilt. You can find a photograph of this quilt on page 75.

That was the beginning of what is now an extensive inspiration file. It's filled with photos of colorful room settings, floral arrangements, and landscapes I've clipped from newspapers and magazines. Whenever I need an idea for a color scheme, I go through my file of goodies until I find a picture with an arrangement of colors that appeals to me. (The color scheme for the quilt on page 76 was inspired by a magazine photo of a vase filled with luscious peach and red-violet roses.) I also like to buy sale-priced art, gardening, and photography books. The wildly eccentric palettes of Van Gogh and the soft color-impressions of Monet have inspired many of my quilts.

Lesson Five gives you more creative leeway than previous lessons. You will be making all the fabric choices and deciding how much of each fabric to purchase. You will also be responsible for creating an original border to enhance your design.

Begin by choosing a picture or photograph with a combination of colors so appealing that you practically start salivating! If you don't come across anything in a book or magazine, look around your house; perhaps you will find a painting or an "object d'art" (like a china plate or bowl) that's inspiring. The picture or object you select will be the source of your color scheme for this lesson.

I've chosen the Sunshine and Shadows pattern for this exercise. It's a classic early American design, but the movement back and forth between light and dark values can make a quilt look like a piece of abstract art or a colorful mosaic of tiles. The overall design of the pattern gives you the opportunity to create an enticing exploration of color and fabric personalities.

Supplies
■ Basic supplies only (page 7)

inspiration

any stimulus to creative thought or action...

THE FABRICS

Look at the picture or object you've selected and make a list of all the colors you can see. Then decide what kinds of fabric prints will best interpret the feeling of your inspirational subject. I chose the oriental vase shown at the right. The surface is decorated with birds, flowers, and leaves, so when I was interviewing fabrics I tried to find prints that would echo those textures. Before you start choosing fabrics, spend a few moments deciding what it is about the combination of colors in your inspirational source that excites you, then make a conscious effort to choose fabrics that reflect this enthusiasm.

Inspirational Source

When you look at the quilt design diagram below, you will notice there are a total of seventeen fabric positions. First go through your fabric collection for likely candidates and then go shopping. You probably won't need more than an eighth yard of any individual fabric to complete the design. The number of fabrics should depend on the variety of colors represented in your inspirational source. For design continuity, it's a good idea to repeat a few of the fabrics. I used fourteen different fabrics to complete my design.

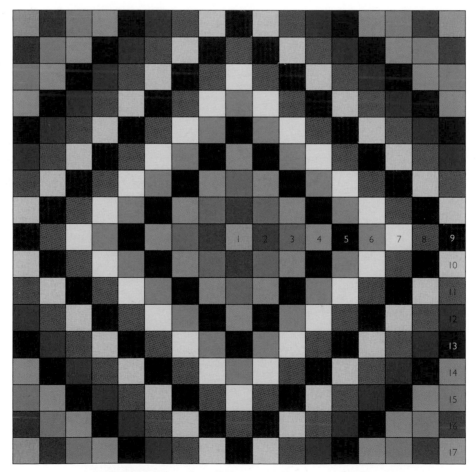

Quilt Design Diagram

BEGIN THE DESIGN

To paste-up, or not to paste-up: that is the question. I fully intended to make a mock-up of my quilt on 8 x 8 graph paper (using rough-cut ½" squares and a glue stick), but with all my beautiful new fabrics spread out in front of me, I couldn't resist starting the actual design. I began by cutting a 2" x 44"-45" strip across the width of each fabric. I placed the strips in front of me and attempted to arrange them in the order I thought they might be used. (At this point, it was just an educated guess.) I cut one 2" square from the #1 fabric and placed it in the middle of my design board. Next, I cut four 2" squares from the #2 fabric and placed them around the first square. I continued cutting and placing squares on my design board until I reached the #9 position at the edge of the quilt, then I started working toward the four corners. I cut some squares from the rest of the fabrics and repeated a few I had used before. Note: I cut additional 2" strips and squares as needed.

This is going to be a "trial and error" process and you will probably do a lot of rearranging before you are satisfied with the final design.

GENERAL DESIGN SUGGESTIONS

- Study your inspirational source. If one or two colors are dominant, make them dominant in your quilt. If there are more warm colors than cool colors, reflect this tendency in your design.

- Work from the center of the quilt to the outside edge. Put one square of the darkest, lightest, or brightest fabric in the middle of your design board in the #1 position.

- Work back and forth from warm to cool colors and include value movement within some of the color groups. (Note: Value movement means to place lighter and darker values of the same color next to each other.) Doing this will give a shimmering effect to the finished quilt.

- Consider putting a dark value color in the #9 position; it will act as an interior frame and form a dramatic visual diamond.

- You might try designing just one quarter of the quilt to see if the prints you have chosen are working well together and if there is a good movement of color and value.

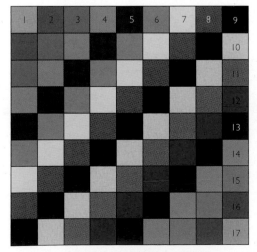

One Quarter of the Design Diagram

CRITIQUE

When all the squares are in place, analyze your design.

■ Does your quilt project the feeling and mood of the subject?

■ Is there a dramatic visual movement of color and value?

■ Is there enough contrast?

■ Do you like it?

When you can answer yes to all four questions, sew the squares together.

SEWING INSTRUCTIONS

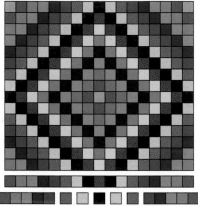

Quilt Construction Diagram

Start at the bottom row and sew the squares together using the method described on page 103 in the Sewing Notes chapter. Press all the seam allowances toward the left. Sew the squares together in the row directly above the bottom row and press all the seam allowances toward the right. Continue sewing rows of squares together, alternating the pressing direction of the seam allowances. When all the squares are sewn into rows, join the rows. Press all the seam allowances either up or down.

BORDERS

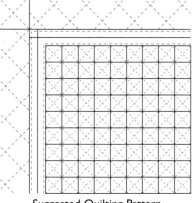

Suggested Quilting Pattern

If this were a perfect world, I would have found an oriental style print that exactly mirrored the decoration and colors on the vase. But I didn't, so I created a border that I felt complimented my quilt. The border design I chose may not be right for your quilt. Perhaps you will decide to use only one fabric, perhaps more. And don't hesitate to introduce an entirely new fabric for the border. Most of the time I prefer to make the border with a fabric that doesn't appear anywhere else in the quilt. Quilt and finish as desired.

CONCLUSION

What you should have learned from this lesson is that you are perfectly capable of creating an absolutely gorgeous color scheme. All you need to do is select a source of inspiration that is rich with color and professionally rendered. That means executed by an accomplished artist, decorator, or photographer. Start your inspiration file today and let the professionals do the color work. All you have to do is interpret their genius with a collection of fabrics. What could be easier!

Quilt Gallery

Hing Chan, Castro Valley, California ▲
Inspiration: Children's book illustration

Glenna Valley, Lafayette, California ▲
Inspiration: Photograph of pansies

Pamela Edwards, Santa Clara, California ▲
Inspiration: Photograph of a braided rug

Barbara Beck, Orinda, California ▲
Inspiration: Decorative plate

five

Shades of Tiffany, ©Gai Perry, 1997, 47" x 47" ▲

One of my enduring, and as yet unsatisfied, passions is to own a piece of artwork created by Louis Comfort Tiffany. For me, his artistry with stained glass is the ultimate color experience. One day I was thumbing through the pages of a glitzy coffee table book about Tiffany and decided I couldn't resist owning some of those brilliant transparent colors one minute longer. I had to make a stained glass quilt.

I chose the colors on a glowing Tiffany lampshade as my inspiration and made a quilt using an original "crystal" pattern. I added just enough narrow strips of black to suggest stained glass leading, but not enough to interfere with the vibrant interplay of color-on-color in the main body of the quilt.

East of the Sun and West of the Moon, Gai Perry, 1986, 41" x 41" ▲

My favorite childhood book was a collection of Norwegian fairy tales called *East of the Sun and West of the Moon*. The illustrations were done by a brilliant artist named Kay Nielsen. With palettes of mauve, peach, copper, navy, black, emerald, and cream, he painted romantic scenes of damsels on horseback, villainous trolls, and enchanted kingdoms. Though the colors for this quilt were originally inspired by an oriental screen, when the top was finished, it was so reminiscent of Neilsen's artwork that I named it in honor of the book and designed stars, waves, and interlocking moons for the quilting pattern.

It's All About Balance, Gai Perry, 1988, 72" x 72" ▲

The colors in this Philadelphia Pavement pattern were inspired by a photograph in a needlepoint book. The picture featured a collection of blue and white porcelain bowls filled with extravagantly colored yellow, pink, and coral roses.

On page 11 of the Color Notes chapter I mentioned that it takes two or three times as much of a cool color to balance the impact of a warm color. This quilt is proof of that statement. Even though the cool colors occupy much more space, one gets a sense of equal proportion between the warm and cool elements.

LESSON siX

My Granddaughter, Carly, At Age Five, Gai Perry, 20½" × 24½" ▲

Carly is a child of summer. She likes strawberries,
juicy red watermelon and bright flowers.
Her favorite colors are pink and purple...and she can't
resist playing in pools, ponds, and puddles.
Carly's hair is the color of taffy candy and she is feminine
to the core—no ball playing or rough games for her.
Carly has lots of friends and they have tea parties on her
sunny front lawn. She is the girl in the polka dot dress.
My granddaughter has a great capacity for love, which encompasses
her family, animals, and surprisingly, bugs.

I'm concerned about the day to day lives of our children. When they aren't in school or day care, they spend their time watching TV, playing video games, or working with a computer. When do they get a chance to dream, or to just sit and listen while someone reads from a storybook without pictures? How are they going to learn to use their imagination or visualize fantasies and fairy tales? Now that I think about it, adults are exposed to these same kinds of mind-numbing experiences. Are we in danger of losing the ability to envision a landscape or create a mind picture? Let's find out!

In the previous lesson, you built a color scheme using an object, photograph, or painting as your reference. Now I want you to explore your imagination to find a set of colors that will illustrate a person, place, or thing that is important to you. You will focus on the subject and take a memory picture. Then you will interpret this memory picture with a collection of prints and solid color fabrics.

As you work on this lesson, you will find yourself becoming very close to your subject. When the quilt is finished and hanging on the wall, you'll be pleasantly reminded of the subject every time you look at it. Now don't feel intimidated. I'm going to take you by the hand and lead you through every step.

Supplies
- Basic supplies (page 7)
- Pencil and paper

The pattern I've chosen for this lesson uses just one size triangle. I saw this arrangement years ago in a book of Amish crib quilts and I think it offers good possibilities for creating a contemporary abstract design.

Begin by choosing a subject. It could be a person with whom you are familiar, like a husband or close relative, or it could be a special event or a location that has left you with a strong impression. Here are some ideas:

family member	vacation trip	your garden
holiday	childhood memory	family reunion
secret place	special keepsake	pet
memorable event	geographic location	magical moment

Visualization

to form a mental image…

Once you've chosen the subject for your memory picture, it's important to know that the impressions and color choices are yours to make. There is no right or wrong. Here's an example of what I'm talking about: Several years ago, I taught a class in which two students both chose the ocean as their subject. One of them planned to interpret the Atlantic Ocean off the coast of Maine; the other was going to do the Pacific Ocean surrounding the Hawaiian Islands. The finished quilts were strikingly different. The Atlantic was done in soft foggy grays, dull greens, dark blues, and white. The Pacific was shimmering with sunlight golds, brilliant blues, and tropical turquoise.

The following paragraph is a practice exercise. Read it, then visualize the scene. Focus on the different elements and try to see the colors with your mind's eye. Notice that I don't give any descriptive color references. You will have to supply them.

At the top of this memory picture is an endless panorama of summer sky.

Here and there, snow capped mountains fade into the distance.

Beneath the mountains is a forest of tall pine trees.

There is a meadow in the foreground, dotted with wildflowers and quiet places.

A sparkling stream wanders along the edge of the meadow, casting reflections of summer sunlight.

The scene is peaceful and serene.

Get a pencil and paper and make a list of all the colors you can visualize in this memory picture. Here are the colors that came to me when I visualized the scene. Your set of colors will be different because, as I said before, no two people interpret color in exactly the same way.

Sky: brilliant azure blue and turquoise, maybe some touches of white

Mountains: snowy white mixed with shades of pale mauve, violet, and light blue

Pine Forest: dark rich greens and blue-greens

Meadow: bright green dappled with yellow-green and a sprinkling of pink, red, yellow, and blue for the wildflowers

Stream: a reflection of the sky, sparkled with sunlight

six

THE FABRICS

Once your subject is chosen, sit in a comfortable chair, close your eyes, and focus on your memory picture. If it's a person, what color clothes does he or she wear? What are his or her hobbies? Is this person bigger than life or quiet and introspective? Try to visualize their character, as well as their physical appearance. When you have formulated your impressions, make a list of the colors and kinds of theme prints you may want to use. Now go through your fabric collection and pull out prints and solids that will help you build your memory picture. Plan on using at least fifteen fabrics. (You only need a few 3¼" squares from each.)

There are all sorts of wonderful fabrics available today to help you design your quilt. Look for flower garden prints and wood grained fabrics. Find prints that give the impression of elements like water, sky, and trees. Theme prints with specific images can also help you interpret your subject.

BEGIN THE DESIGN

Once your fabrics are assembled, cut three 3¼" squares from each piece. Cut each square diagonally into two triangles. (Note: There is no point in making alternate grain triangles for this lesson because you don't know, at this point, where the triangles will be placed.) Using the quilt diagram below as your reference, start arranging the triangles on your design board. Study the examples on page 85 for ideas. The arrangement of the triangles is entirely your choice. You can put them in horizontal rows of one fabric per row, or you can totally mix up the colors and prints, creating a more abstract effect. If you want to interpret an outdoor scene, start at the top of the quilt and put in the fabric for the sky; then work your way toward the bottom.

Quilt Design Diagram

If you don't know how to get started, just arbitrarily pick up four triangles from one of the fabrics and arrange them across the top of your design board. Then choose three triangles from a different fabric and place them in the spaces the first triangles have created. Ask yourself if the second fabric looks attractive with the first fabric. Is there a good contrast? (warm-cool colors, value range, different print scale, etc.) Now select three triangles from a third fabric and place them directly beneath the second set of triangles. Refer to the example sequence below. Continue putting up triangles and eventually something will happen to jump-start your imagination. As your design takes shape, you will probably need to cut more triangles. Try not to let yourself feel discouraged; this may be the first time you've ever made a quilt without any kind of visual reference. Most of you will know intuitively when the design work is finished. You will have become totally immersed in the visualization and have a wonderful sense of familiarity with your subject.

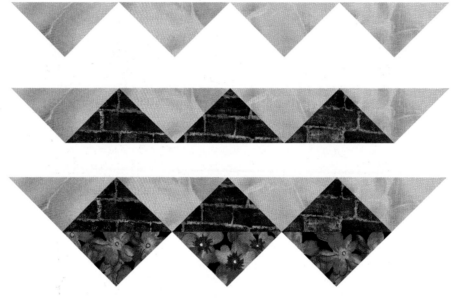

How to Begin the Design
These prints might suggest the beginning of a brick-walled garden.

CRITIQUE

Stand away from the design board and analyze your design.
- Look for a nice balance of colors and textures.
- Does the quilt really represent your subject?
- Can you look at each fabric and know what it contributes to your memory picture?
- Finally, does it succeed as a good piece of abstract design? (Note: This is a trick question because there are really no definitive criteria for judging a good abstract design. If you have managed to combine a powerful arrangement of colors, contrast, and textures—and your heart goes "pitty-pat" when you look at your quilt—then I'd judge it a success.)

When we critique these quilts in class I ask each person to describe what the individual fabrics mean. Often the description sounds like a free verse poem. You may want to write it down and include it with your quilt. Perhaps you could have it photo-transferred to the backing fabric.

SEWING INSTRUCTIONS

This quilt will first be sewn in diagonal rows. Start at the lower left-hand corner and sew the two corner triangles together. Press the seam allowance toward the left. Move up to the next diagonal row and sew the opposing triangles into two square units and press all the seam allowances toward the right. Sew the newly created squares together and add the two perimeter triangles. Press all seam allowances in this row toward the right. Sew the triangles in the next row into square units and press all the seam allowances toward the left. Join the squares and perimeter triangles and press all the seam allowances toward the left. Continue in this manner, alternating the pressing direction from row to row. When all the squares and triangles are sewn into diagonal strips, sew the strips together. Choose a direction and press all the seam allowances either up or down.

Quilt Construction Diagram

BORDERS

The width and number of borders is your choice to make. Sometimes these visualization quilts look better without an inner border but if you think an inner border will relate to your subject and help finish telling the story, then include one. Also, put a nice wide outer border on this quilt, perhaps as wide as 4½". It will make an interesting area for some personalized quilting patterns. The quilting design I put on *Santa Fe* (shown on page 85) definitely enhances the overall look of the quilt. The pattern was inspired by the design on a Navajo silver bracelet I'd purchased while visiting that town a number of years ago. Quilt and finish as desired.

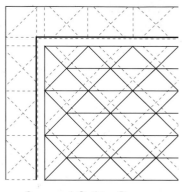

Suggested Quilting Pattern

CONCLUSIONS

The ability to see pictures with our minds is a treasured gift, but if we don't exercise it once in a while I'm afraid we'll lose it. Before tackling the design of your next quilt, try to visualize the finished product with your mind's eye. Close your eyes and see the harmony of the colors and the dramatic contrast between the light and dark areas. Perhaps this exercise will help to define your vision; perhaps not, but it couldn't hurt to try!

Quilt Gallery

The Grand Canyon, Laurel Samberg, ▲
Walnut Creek, California

Fourth of July At Lake Tahoe, Glenna Valley ▲
Lafayette, California

Daughter's Twenty-first Birthday, Karen Garret, ▲
Union City, California

Santa Fe, Gai Perry, Walnut Creek, California ▲

six

Field and Stream, Gai Perry, 1996, 33" x 41" ▲

This quilt takes a realist rather than an abstract approach to the visualization lesson. It also comes with an interesting story. I wrote the paragraph describing the mountain scene (on page 80) in 1987, when I first started teaching these color lessons. In 1990 I began developing my Impressionist Landscape series and put the color classes on hold. From then on, I devoted all my time to designing landscape quilts, teaching the technique, and eventually writing two books.

In 1996, I designed Field and Stream, and don't you think it's a perfect visual description of the paragraph I wrote eleven years earlier? It's almost spooky! I didn't put this coincidence together until I began teaching color classes again and read through my old notes. I had completely forgotten the paragraph but, obviously, it was still floating around somewhere in my subconscious. Now I'm beginning to wonder if this visualization lesson was the catalyst that launched the Impressionist Landscape series. If you are curious about this landscape technique, you will find my books listed in the Bibliography, on page 111.

Fission Star, Gai Perry, 1988, 67" x 67" ▲

To get into the mood, and with only the vaguest feeling of what I wanted this quilt to look like, I played a "new age" tape and let my imagination drift toward the farthest reaches of outer space. I visualized a giant star that was ready to explode—shooting fragments of debris across the galaxy. As I listened to the music I began to draw the quilt to scale on graph paper. I used four Tree of Life blocks, minus the trunks, to form the center star and repeated segments of the star as I worked toward the four corners of the design. *Fission Star* demonstrates how a basic technique like visualization can lead to a larger and more important quilt.

Gemstones and River Rocks, Gai Perry, 1998 27½" x 41½" ▲

I had already made a quilt visualizing a person and a place; now I wanted to make a quilt visualizing an object. One night, before going to bed, I made a list of several "things" I like. The next morning I awoke thinking about the smooth texture of polished river rocks and the luster of gemstones like amethyst and turquoise. To design my quilt, I gathered an assortment of contemporary batiks and rock-oriented theme prints. I used the same size triangle as required for the lesson quilt, but increased the count.

LESSON seven

Artist-Conceived Nine-Patch, Gai Perry, 41³/₄" x 50¹/₄" ▲

I don't paint very often anymore, but when I do it's because something has touched me so deeply, I feel compelled to put the image on canvas. I start by observing the subject; gathering impressions of mood, shape, and environment. Then I choose my palette of colors. I use a pencil to sketch the entire picture on my canvas. This preliminary mapping allows me to nudge all the elements into a graceful balance. When the sketch is finished, I lay in the background colors, giving careful thought to the interaction of patterns and textures. The last step is to paint in the small details and to add the highlights and shadows. These are the finishing touches that will make my picture come alive.

The purpose of this final lesson is to design a quilt using the same techniques I've just described. As you develop this quilt, keep in mind all you have learned from the previous lessons:

- Use a generous number of fabrics.
- Enrich the color scheme with several tints, tones, and shades from your chosen palette.
- Include light, medium, and dark value prints.
- Employ at least three kinds of contrast.
- Select an assortment of fabric patterns and print scales.
- Choose fabrics that reinforce the style and personality of your quilt.

Supplies

- Basic supplies only (page 7)

THE FABRICS

You will be making a crib-size quilt using a variation of the classic nine-patch pattern. Start by purchasing one yard of a beautifully colored print. (If you want the print to run in one direction only, get one and a third yards.) From now on, this print will be referred to as the subject of your quilt and it will eventually be used for the border. The print must talk to you—it should really "knock your socks off." The design capabilities will be enhanced if you choose a multicolored fabric with a combination of warm and cool hues.

Once your subject fabric is chosen, analyze its personality. If you need to refresh your memory on how to do this, reread the Fabric Notes chapter beginning on page 16. When you feel familiar with your subject, select six background prints. These prints should represent the six most dominant colors in your subject. They should also reflect the personality of the subject fabric. If you have chosen an ethnic-style print, for example, the background prints should maintain a similar character. Consider fabrics that will provide contrast of color, value, scale, and pattern.

I would suggest starting with quarter yard cuts of fabrics A through F, as noted on the nine-patch diagram. After you have started the design, and determined which fabric will be used for each position, you can get additional yardage for the D and E squares. Hold off buying anything for the scrap nine-patches until after the background fabrics are cut and put in place.

Nine-Patch Diagram

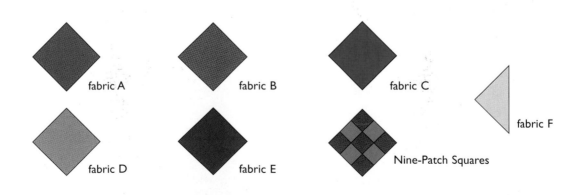

fabric A

fabric B

fabric C

fabric F

fabric D

fabric E

Nine-Patch Squares

BEGIN THE DESIGN

The nine-patch diagram represents your sketch of the overall picture (or in this case, the nine-patch quilt). You will start the design by laying in the background fabrics. It's a good idea to fold the subject fabric into eighths (lengthwise) to simulate a border strip, then pin it along the far right edge of your design board. This will help you to determine if the background fabrics you have chosen are appropriate. Now you have to make preliminary decisions about which print to put in what position. Bear in mind that you can always shift the position of a print as you are designing.

step 1   Cut five 3½" squares from fabric A and two 3½" squares from fabric C. Place the squares in a vertical point-to-point column, down the center of your design board.

step 2   Cut fourteen 3½" squares from fabric B. Place the squares in two point-to-point vertical columns, one on each side of the middle row. Be sure to leave space for the nine-patches, which will be added later.

step 3   Cut fourteen 3½" squares from fabric C. Place the squares in two point-to-point vertical columns as shown in the above diagram.

step 4   Cut twenty-four 3½" squares from fabric D and place them in the order shown in the above diagram.

step 5 Cut twenty-eight 3½" squares from fabric E and place them in the order shown in the diagram.

step 6 Cut twenty-eight 3⅞" triangles from fabric F and place them around the perimeter of the design. Refer to the Quilt Construction Diagram on page 92 for placement. Note: Sometimes I choose just one print for these triangles, other times I choose several prints with approximately the same value and color. Doing it this way gives the quilt a scrappier look. To quick-cut the perimeter triangles, cut seven 5½" squares and cut each one diagonally twice into four triangles. Cut two 3" squares and then cut them diagonally in half for the four corner triangles.

Now that the background fabrics for your quilt are in place, you must decide if the combination of colors and fabric personalities is pleasing. Ask the following questions:

- Do the background colors reflect the personality of the subject fabric?
- Is there a variety of print scales and patterns?
- Are the fabrics attractively arranged or do some of the square positions need to be shifted?

When you feel secure with the background of your quilt, it's time to put in the highlights and shadows (all the scrap nine-patches). Still using your subject fabric as a guide for color and fabric style, choose several light, medium, and dark prints. Hopefully, you will find everything you need in your fabric collection. You can exaggerate the colors and values; meaning you can pick fabrics with colors that are slightly brighter or duller, and darker or lighter than those in your subject fabric. This will give the nine-patches some added sparkle.

step 7 Cut five 1½" squares of a darker-value print and four 1½" squares of a lighter-value print and place them on the design board in any one of the spaces that have been reserved for the nine-patches. Continue cutting 1½" squares and build combinations of five darker and four lighter prints. The more you design, the braver you'll get. Make sure to mix up the color groups and pair warm colors with cool ones.

Try not to make more than three nine-patches with the exact same combination of fabrics and don't use any of the background fabrics.

step 8 When all the nine-patches are in place, sew them into 3½" squares and put them back on the design board. To sew the nine-patches: Stitch the three top squares together and press seam allowances toward the left. Stitch the middle three squares together and press seam allowances toward the right. Stitch the bottom three squares together and press seam allowances toward the left. Join the three rows and press all the seam allowances either up or down.

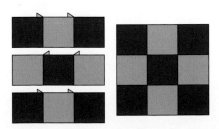

Sewing the Nine-Patches

CRITIQUE

- Check to see that the arrangement of the nine-patches enhances the overall look of the quilt. Perhaps some will need to be switched in order to ensure a balance of color.

- Does your quilt have the feeling of a tapestry? What I mean is, are all the colors and prints beautifully integrated, with no particular area catching more attention than another?

- Does the main body of the quilt still reflect the personality and style of the border fabric?

SEWING INSTRUCTIONS

The quilt will be sewn into diagonal strips and then the strips will be joined together. Start at the lower left-hand corner and sew the square to the two perimeter triangles. Press all the seam allowances toward the left. Sew the next diagonal strip of squares and perimeter triangles and press all the seam allowances toward the right. Continue in this manner and alternate the pressing direction of the seam allowances in each strip. When all the rows are sewn into strips, sew them together. Choose a pressing direction and press all the seam allowances either up or down.

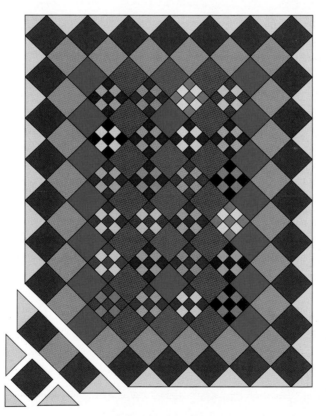

Quilt Construction Diagram

BORDERS

The lesson quilt has a 1" wide inner border, a middle border measuring ¾", and a 4" wide outer border. (Note: These are finished measurements.) It isn't necessary to copy this arrangement exactly. Let the width of the pattern-repeat on your subject fabric dictate the width of your border.

This won't happen often, but once in a while, after the main body of your quilt is sewn, you might decide the print you selected for your subject (and the final border) doesn't feel right. Either your design statement is complete without a border or a different fabric now seems more appropriate. Don't despair. Congratulate yourself on the fact that you have developed the ability to make this kind of artistic decision. Choose another fabric for the border or leave it unbordered. The subject fabric can be used for the backing—that way you won't have to feel guilty about not putting it on the front. Quilt and finish as desired.

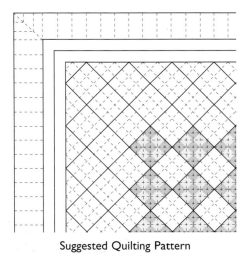

Suggested Quilting Pattern

CONCLUSION

When I first developed this pattern, I found it irresistible and couldn't stop making "just one more." I made them as baby gifts, wallhangings, and couch throws. I kept altering the pattern. Sometimes I made four-patches instead of nine-patches and occasionally I changed the arrangement of the background squares. Sometimes, as I mentioned above, I omitted the final border. Once you become familiar with the layout, you can improvise to your heart's content.

This quilt design can be enlarged or reduced. Here is the formula:

For nine-patch quilts, make the finished size of the alternate squares divisible by three. Make the nine-patches one-third the size of the finished alternate squares. Add the ½" measurement for seam allowances *after* determining the finished size of the large and small squares.

For four-patches, make the finished size of the alternate squares divisible by two. Make the four-patches one half the size of the finished alternate squares. Add the ½" measurement for the seam allowances *after* determining the finished size of the large and small squares.

Quilt Gallery

◄ Favorite Colors, Weebee Brown, Orinda, California

When the main body of Weebee's quilt was sewn, it looked much brighter and more colorful than her subject fabric, so she did exactly as I suggested: she chose another border print and used her original selection for the backing fabric.

A Spring Garden, Joyce Lytle, San Ramon, California ►

Joyce's subject fabric is the bright green floral print in the D position. She chose to put it in the main body of the quilt rather than using it for the border. Her border print has sentimental value. It's an older fabric that originally came from her parents' department store.

Ya Gotta Love Pink!, Gai Perry, 1998, 41" x 51". Machine quilted by June Bell ▲

This vintage style quilt was made with a manufacturer's collection of coordinated fabrics. I added a few unrelated prints to slightly brighten the mellow color scheme. Several years ago I made a quilt using a group of coordinated fabrics exclusively and I couldn't figure out why my quilt looked so dull. As I gained experience, I learned that adding a few unpredictable prints will give a quilt more personality and character.

Celadon, Gai Perry, 1998, 38" x 46". Machine quilted by June Bell ▲

When I present this nine-patch lesson in class, I ask students to pick a subject fabric with a variety of colors and some warm-cool contrast. Sometimes what a student chooses isn't particularly colorful, in my opinion, and I always wonder if I have been clear enough with my instructions. It has taken me a while to get it, but I finally realized that not everybody has the same degree of color tolerance. For some people, a border fabric with several bright hues appears too intense, even unattractive. So the question is: How does one make a quilt look compelling and lively with a limited palette? The answer is: By using an interesting variety of contrasting prints. To prove this, I made *Celadon*.

Diamond Field, Gai Perry, 1989, 51" x 63" ▲

This pattern is a variation of the lesson quilt and it was originally intended to be a composition in red and blue-green. I had all the background squares cut and positioned on my design wall, but I wasn't satisfied with the way the quilt was developing, so I took a photograph to see if I could figure out what was wrong. The picture helped me to see that the values of the two main fabrics were too close to be interesting. I took off all the blue-green squares and began playing with a light tan fabric. The large scale floral fabric I'd chosen for the final border ended up being cut into squares to form the overlapping diamonds in the center of the quilt.

When you have completed the lessons, your ability to make color and fabric decisions should be seven times greater! From now on, as you begin each new quilt project, make an effort to incorporate everything you have learned from this book. You might even want to copy this page and pin it on a wall in your sewing room as a friendly reminder.

LESSON ONE
Put a greater number of fabrics into your quilts. Remember, if five are good, twenty-five are better, and fifty are even better!

LESSON TWO
Enrich your quilts by using several tints, tones, and shades of each color. Doing this will make your quilts look as though they were designed by an artist.

LESSON THREE
To avoid an overall blurring of colors and fabrics, make sure to include some prints with light, medium, and dark values.

LESSON FOUR
Make an effort to include at least three kinds of contrast.

LESSON FIVE
If you are having a hard time putting a group of colors together, make a reference file and use a color scheme that was created by an expert.

LESSON SIX
Visualize the finished quilt. Work with colors you love and make quilts that are a reflection of your personality.

LESSON SEVEN
Include a variety of fabric patterns and print scales. Always choose fabrics that reinforce the style of the quilt you are designing.

I wasn't raised in a family of accomplished needlework artists and other than taking a required semester of home economics in high school, I'd never been near a sewing machine until I fell in love with quilting. One of the nice things about learning to sew with a quilting teacher (as opposed to a mother or dressmaker) is that I didn't have to unlearn any irrelevant sewing habits. I was a fresh sponge waiting to absorb all the right techniques. At the time, the right techniques included learning how to draft a quilt block and working with templates. Before making a quilt top, I had to draw the desired block on graph paper and make plastic templates. This process may sound tedious, but in fact, it was very liberating. It allowed me to become familiar with the block; to feel as though I owned it. By using templates to cut out squares and triangles, I was able to spend more time contemplating a fabric's color and pattern.

I'd been quilting for about five years when the rotary cutter was introduced and all the rules were turned upside down. No more drafting, no more templates, and in my opinion, much of the art was lost. Rotary cutters make cutting too easy. I can almost hear you saying, "Is this girl crazy? What does she mean, too easy!" Let me explain. With a rotary cutter, a quarter yard of fabric can be sliced so fast, and the amount of required pieces attained so quickly, the temptation is to use fewer fabrics. Sometimes quilts made with this cutting method can look mass-produced and unimaginative.

Now that I've said my piece, let's talk about sewing. First, I want to repeat the suggestion to invest in a good basic quilting book. You will find recommendations on page 111. What I'm going to share with you in this chapter are some very basic sewing procedures and a few tricks and techniques I've learned over the years.

When I first developed the Impressionist Landscape series, I had to figure out a method for sewing rows of squares together that would automatically keep them in the right order. To my delight, the method I devised works equally well with traditional piecing and it is extremely fast. Essentially you will be chaining both ends of a row toward the middle. It's better to follow the instructions one step at a time rather than reading ahead and trying to figure them out. In other words, the method is "hands-on."

MY METHOD FOR SEWING STRAIGHT ROWS OF SQUARES TOGETHER

step 1 Begin by putting one pin in the left side of the first square on the left. This will be called unit 1. Now put two pins in the right side of the farthest right square in the row. This will be called unit 2.

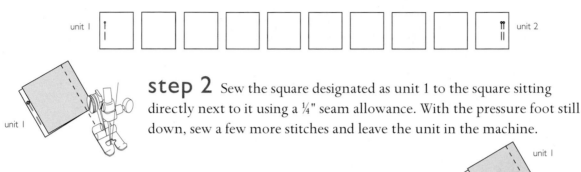

step 2 Sew the square designated as unit 1 to the square sitting directly next to it using a ¼" seam allowance. With the pressure foot still down, sew a few more stitches and leave the unit in the machine.

step 3 From the other end of the same row, pick up the square designated as unit 2 and sew it to the square directly next to it. With the pressure foot still down, sew a few more stitches and leave the unit in the machine. With your scissors, detach unit 1.

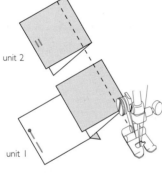

step 4 Move back to the left side of the row, pick up the next square in sequence, and sew it to unit 1. With the pressure foot still down, sew a few more stitches and then leave this unit in the machine. With your scissors, detach unit 2.

step 5 Move back to the right side of the row and pick up the next square in sequence and sew it to unit 2. With the pressure foot still down, sew a few more stitches and this leave this unit in the machine. With your scissors, detach unit 1.

step 6 Continue sewing in this manner until all the squares in the row are joined to the first or second unit. Sew the two units together and pin the resulting strip on the design board in the correct position. Note: This method also works for diagonal rows of squares and triangles. Put the pins in the perimeter triangles.

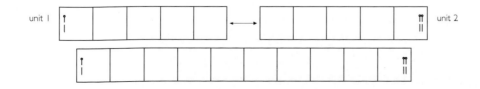

MAKING TRIANGLES

I can't say this strongly enough! Cut triangles accurately and, wherever possible, sew a straight grain edge to a bias edge to keep the unit from stretching. Instructions on how to accomplish this are included in Lessons Two and Three. Once two triangles are joined together, unless otherwise indicated, always press toward the darkest value triangle and then clip off the points. Doing this will help to make your piecing more accurate and, later on, easier to hand quilt.

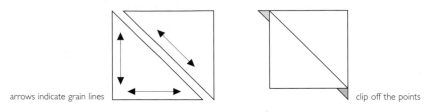

arrows indicate grain lines   clip off the points

PRESSING

Press as you sew! Press triangles after stitching them into squares. Press each row of squares (or squares and triangles) before joining them to the next row. Careful and prodigious pressing will result in quilt tops that are flat and "in square." I keep a large terry cloth bath towel spread across the top of my ironing board cover. I do all my pressing on this towel because it helps to prevent all those nasty little seam allowance ridges from showing through on the front of the quilt.

Whether or not you use steam when pressing, try not to overwork the fabric by constantly wiggling the iron back and forth. Put the iron straight down on the item you are pressing, hold it for a second or two, then gently move on.

BORDERS

The border fabric is an important element because it should define and enhance the character of the quilt it surrounds. I have always had a difficult time choosing borders. I can combine forty or fifty prints in the main body of a quilt with relative ease, but when it comes to deciding on the perfect border, I can turn into a quivering mass of indecision. It's kind of like picking a fabric for a sofa. There's so much to choose from and having to commit to just one fabric can be a traumatic experience.

I have solved this problem by giving myself permission to take a border off if I don't like it, and to start over again. Once I had to redo a border three times before I was satisfied. My rationalization is that I will eventually use the discarded fabric for something else. I'm telling you this because I want you to know that even the most experienced quilters can have trouble making color and design choices.

It has always been my opinion that folk art, country-style, and scrap quilts (the kinds of quilts found in this book) look more in character with straight borders. On the other hand, formal quilts like a broderie perse or an elegant appliqué are enhanced with borders that have been mitered. Landscape and pictorial quilts will also look better with mitered borders because they perform the function of a frame. All the lesson quilts should live quite comfortably with straight borders, unless you have a strong opinion otherwise.

Attaching Straight Borders

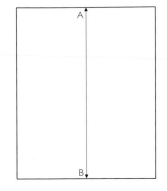

step 1 Carefully press the quilt top and lay it on a flat surface. With a ruler or measuring tape, determine the distance between points A and B. (Note: It's best to measure from the center top to the center bottom, because this is where the quilt will be the narrowest. Generally there tends to be a little stretching along the outer edges.

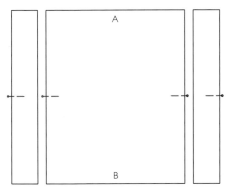

step 2 Fold the border fabric selvage to selvage and then fold again. This will give you four layers to cut through. (The exception is Lesson Seven, which will use the length of the fabric.) Place the folded fabric on the cutting mat. Cut four strips the desired width of the border. Cut two of the four strips to the exact measurement of the length between A and B. Put a pin in the right and left center edges of the quilt top and a pin in the center of each of the two border strips.

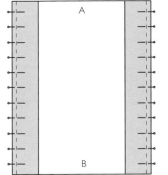

step 3 Match the pins and attach the border strips to the center points of the quilt top with the right sides facing the quilt. Now pin the ends of the border strips to each corner of the quilt top. Fill in between the center and the corners with more pins. Ease if necessary. Sew the two border strips to the quilt top and press the seam allowances away from the quilt. (Remove pins as necessary.)

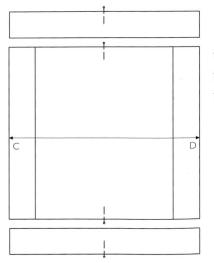

step 4 Measure the distance between points C and D and cut the two remaining border strips to that exact length. Put a pin in the top and bottom center edges of the quilt top and another pin in the center point of each of the two border strips, then repeat step 3.

BACKING

Once your quilt top is finished and carefully pressed, it's time to give it the supple texture and coziness that comes with quilting. First you will need to choose a backing fabric. I like to use a print that will compliment the style and theme of the quilt top. I also like the print to be busy enough to hide any quilting flaws. The backing fabric should be larger than the quilt top by at least five inches in the length and width. With larger quilts, this will require some piecing.

BATTING

Most quilters will develop a preference for a particular type of batting. My favorite battings are Mountain Mist® Quilt Light® (a synthetic) and Fairfield Soft Touch® (100% cotton). Both of these battings are thin and make the finished quilt look smooth and flat. They are also easy to "needle."

PREPARING THE QUILT SANDWICH

Basting your quilt requires a large flat surface, so the first thing you need to do is clear the piles of clutter from your dining room table. Once this is accomplished, cover the table with one of those quadruple-fold dressmaker's boards. It protects the table and is large enough to accommodate the lesson quilts. (For larger quilts, I tape two of these fold-out boards together.)

After you press the backing fabric, spread it over the dressmaker's board (right side facing down) and put pieces of masking tape here and there around the perimeter to keep it nice and tight. Next in this quilt sandwich comes the batting. Smooth the batting to eliminate folds and wrinkles and then cover it with your quilt top. Make sure the right side of the quilt top is facing up.

If you are hand quilting, use straight pins, placed about every four inches, to temporarily secure the layers. For machine quilting, use #1 nickel-plated safety pins. No further basting is required for machine quilting.

BASTING FOR HAND QUILTING

Once the quilt sandwich is pinned, it can be thread-basted with a radial or grid style pattern. I've discovered that quilters are fiercely loyal to either one method or the other.

After your quilt is basted, remove the masking tape and pins. Fold the excess batting and backing fabric over the front edges of the quilt and baste with a running stitch. This will help to protect the edges from fraying and stretching while you are quilting.

HAND QUILTING

I'm totally committed to the process of hand quilting! For me, it has a calming effect and allows me to reflect on the pursuit of life, love, and creative dinner menus. There are many ways to effectively accomplish a hand quilted project and if you are comfortable with your method, that's fine. This is the way I do it.

I baste my quilts with a radial, rather than a grid pattern. I do this because I quilt in my lap without a hoop. I've found the radial basting keeps the backing fabric from bunching. If you want to try quilting without a hoop, which incidentally is much faster, just remember to start your stitches in the middle section of the quilt and gradually work toward the four corners.

I use 100% cotton quilting thread and sometimes, if I don't want the quilting stitches to be obvious, I change thread color from area to area. Because most of these lesson quilts are fairly small, they are nice projects to carry around with you to work on in spare moments.

MACHINE QUILTING

If you have machine quilted at least one quilt top, then you already know more about the process than I do. It's not that I don't approve of this type of quilting; actually I'm envious of those of you who have mastered the technique. One of these days I'm going to block out enough time to learn, but until then, the most thoughtful advice I can give is: Get Harriet Hargrave's book, *Heirloom Machine Quilting*. It's the best! And if there is a local quilt shop offering a machine quilting class, do yourself a favor and take it.

BINDING THE QUILT

You're almost finished! Just one more decision to make and that is whether or not to bind your quilt with the same fabric you used for the final border. With scrappy looking quilts, I welcome the opportunity to add another element of pattern and color. My favorite kinds of bindings are made with plaids, stripes, or colorful prints that haven't been used anywhere else in the quilt. Sometimes I like to use more than one fabric to bind a quilt, so I prefer to make individual binding strips rather than a continuous binding. I may be a majority of one here, but I also think individual binding strips look neater and more professional.

Before you attach the binding, take your quilt to the ironing board and carefully press it with steam, on a medium-warm polyester setting. Never, never, never use a hot iron. The batting could melt! This procedure is like blocking a sweater; it eliminates any rippling and, somehow, it makes the quilting stitches look better.

Measure your quilt to see if it is still "in square." Sometimes during quilting, the corners become slightly stretched. If this happens, trim them just enough to get the quilt back in square.

Cut four 2" fabric strips in lengths slightly longer than the length and width of the quilt. Fold the strips in half and press. Using ¼" seam allowances, machine stitch the raw edges of two strips to the right and left edges of the quilt. Fold over and hand stitch to the back of the quilt. Repeat the process for the top and bottom edges of the quilt.

I guess I must have a romantic nature because I still love fairy tales and I think even quilt books deserve to have happy endings.

U nfortunately, I can't promise you will live happily ever after and that every quilt you make will be a blue ribbon winner, but please allow this ex-cheerleader to give you a few parting words of encouragement and a hardy pat on the back for finishing all the lessons.

As soon as I put the last stitch in a binding, I practically jump up and do a little dance. Hurrah, I did it! I finished another quilt! For a few moments, I feel smug and self-satisfied—and then my mind wanders toward a new project. What pattern will I make this time? What glorious combination of colors and fabrics will I choose? The possibilities are intoxicating. I can feel the creative process starting to bloom again and I love every minute of it!

I hope you had fun working on the lessons and that you learned how to work a little magic with your favorite colors. I also hope that my book has given you the power to feel good about your quiltmaking accomplishments. You should know that whatever else you are in life, you have also become part artist, part seamstress, and part mathematician. Every time you design a quilt, you are creating a visual expression of your personality and color preferences. The more quilts you make, the more they will come to be recognized as your personal signature and your legacy for future generations.

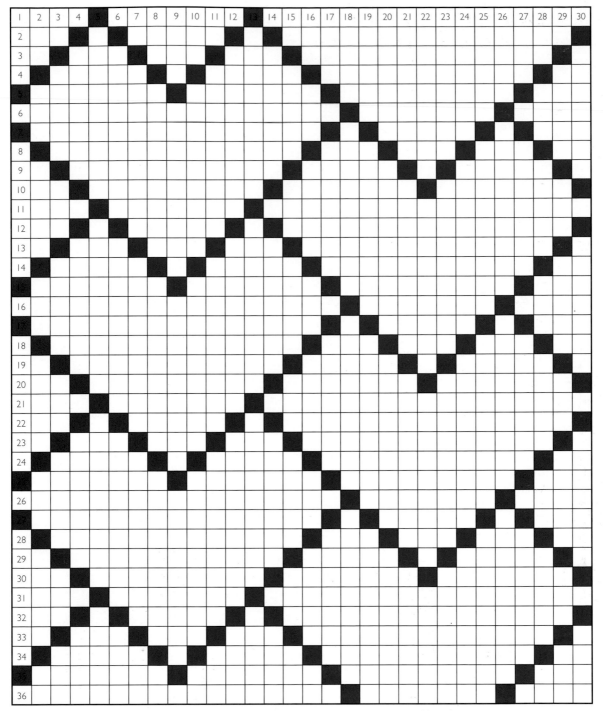

Heart's Delight Quilt Diagram ▲

I debated with myself about how to draw a diagram for this quilt and decided the best way would be simply to show the placement of the red squares that define the nesting hearts. You can choose the fabrics for the rest of the squares by looking at the photo of the quilt or by designing your own interpretation of the pattern. Some of the hearts are filled with a sunshine and shadow arrangement of squares, while others have a scrap, or random, placement. To make this 38" x 45½" quilt, I cut 1¾" squares. Increasing the size of the squares by even a half inch will produce a much larger quilt.

TEMPLATE PATTERNS

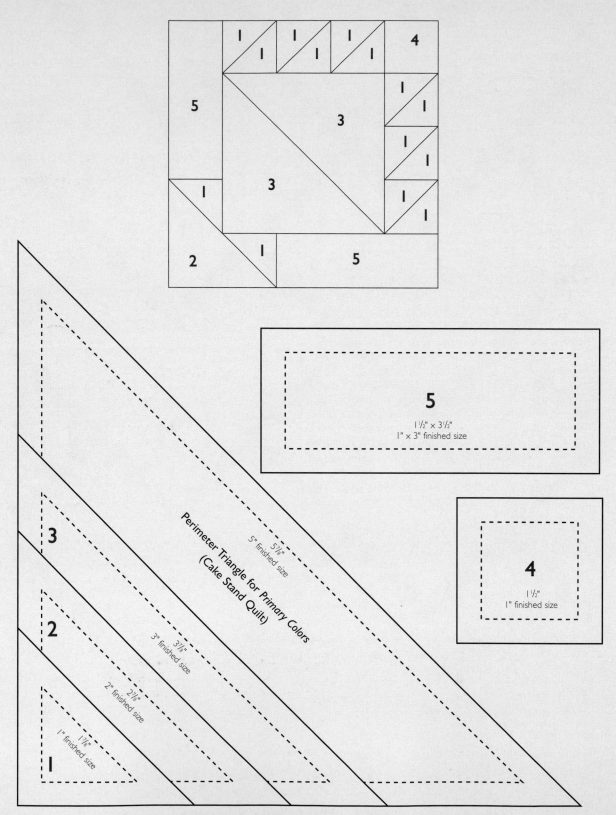

Templates for Lesson Four: Cake Stand Block

COLOR THEORY

Itten, Johannes. *The Elements of Color*. New York: Van Nostrand Reinhold Company, 1970.

Perry, Gai. *Impressionist Palette*. Lafayette, CA: C&T Publishing, 1997.

Perry, Gai. *Impressionist Quilts*. Lafayette, CA: C&T Publishing, 1995.

BASIC QUILTING TECHNIQUES

Hargrave, Harriet. *Heirloom Machine Quilting*. Lafayette, CA: C&T Publishing, 1995.

Leone, Diana. *The New Sampler Quilt*. Lafayette, CA: C&T Publishing, 1993.

McClun, Diana and Laura Nownes. *Quilts! Quilts!! Quilts!!!* Chicago, Ill: The Quilt Digest Press, 1998.

McClun, Diana and Laura Nownes. *Quilts, Quilts, and More Quilts!* Lafayette, CA: C&T Publishing, 1993.

INDEX

ABOUT THE AUTHOR

Gai Perry was introduced to quilting in 1981 and fell head-over-heels in love with this uniquely American craft. She has been a full-time quilter ever since.

In 1985, Gai started teaching and, because of her fondness for early American quilts, her focus was on the effective use of color and fabric in traditional style quilts. By 1990, she had a desire to start painting again, but instead of working with brushes and paint, she developed an original style of quilting she named "The Art of the Impressionist Landscape." She has written two books on the subject.

Now Gai has temporarily returned to traditional quilting to write an exciting new lesson book filled with all kinds of practical and personal information about color and fabric.

Other Books by Gai Perry:

Impressionist Palette

Impressionist Quilts

For more information write for a free catalog from:
C&T Publishing, Inc.
P.O. Box 1456
Lafayette, CA 94549
(800) 284-1114
http://www.ctpub.com
e-mail: ctinfo@ctpub.com

Quilting Supplies
The Cotton Patch Mail Order
3405 Hall Lane, Dept. CTB
Layayette, CA 94549
e-mail: cottonpa@aol.com
(800) 835-4418
(925) 283-7883
A Complete Quilting Supply Store

Other Fine Books From C&T Publishing:

An Amish Adventure, 2nd Edition, Roberta Horton
At Home with Patrick Lose, Colorful Quilted Projects, Patrick Lose
Basic Seminole Patchwork, Cheryl Greider Bradkin
Curves in Motion, Quilt Designs & Techniques, Judy B. Dales
Easy Pieces, Creative Color Play with Two Simple Quilt Blocks, Margaret Miller
Enduring Grace, Quilts from the Shelburne Museum Collection, Celia Y. Oliver
Everything Flowers, Quilts from the Garden, Jean and Valori Wells
Exploring Machine Trapunto, New Dimensions, Hari Walner
The Fabric Makes the Quilt, Roberta Horton
Fancy Appliqué, 12 Lessons to Enhance Your Skills, Elly Sienkiewicz
Freddy's House, Brilliant Color in Quilts, Freddy Moran
Free Stuff for Crafty Kids, Judy Heim and Gloria Hansen
Free Stuff for Quilters on the Internet, 2nd Edition, Judy Heim and Gloria Hansen
Free Stuff for Sewing Fanatics, Judy Heim and Gloria Hansen
Hand Quilting with Alex Anderson, Six Projects for Hand Quilters, Alex Anderson
Heirloom Machine Quilting, Third Edition, Harriet Hargrave
Kaleidoscopes, Wonders of Wonder, Cozy Baker
Make Any Block Any Size, Easy Drawing Method • Unlimited Pattern Possibilities • Sensational Quilt Designs. Joen Wolfrom
Mastering Quilt Marking, Marking Tools and Techniques • Choosing Stencils • Matching Borders & Corners, Pepper Cory
The New England Quilt Museum Quilts, Featuring the Story of the Mill Girls, Jennifer Gilbert
The New Sampler Quilt, Diana Leone
Patchwork Persuasion, Fascinating Quilts from Traditional Designs, Joen Wolfrom

The Photo Transfer Handbook, Snap It, Print It, Stitch It! Jean Ray Laury
Piecing, Expanding the Basics, Ruth B. McDowell
Plaids & Stripes, The Use of Directional Fabrics in Quilts, Roberta Horton
Quilts for Fabric Lovers, Alex Anderson
Quilts from the Civil War, Nine Projects, Historical Notes, Diary Entries, Barbara Brackman
Quilts, Quilts, and More Quilts! Diana McClun and Laura Nownes
Rotary Cutting with Alex Anderson, Tips • Techniques • Projects, Alex Anderson
Say It with Quilts, Diana McClun and Laura Nownes
Scrap Quilts, The Art of Making Do, Roberta Horton
Simply Stars, Quilts that Sparkle, Alex Anderson
Skydyes, A Visual Guide to Fabric Painting, Mickey Lawler
Start Quilting with Alex Anderson, Six Projects for First-Time Quilters, Alex Anderson
Stripes in Quilts, Mary Mashuta
Through the Garden Gate, Quilters and Their Gardens, Jean and Valori Wells
Tradition with a Twist, Variations on Your Favorite Quilts, Blanche Young and Dalene Young Stone
Travels with Peaky and Spike, Doreen Speckmann's Quilting Adventures, Doreen Speckmann
The Visual Dance, Creating Spectacular Quilts, Joen Wolfrom
Wildflowers, Designs for Appliqué and Quilting, Carol Armstrong
Women of Taste, A Collaboration Celebrating Quilt Artists and Chefs, Jen Bilik and Girls Incorporated